P9-DDX-144

MAKING THINGS RIGHT
When Things Go Wrong

DR. PAUL FAULKNER

MAKING THINGS RIGHT When Things Go Wrong

Ten Proven Ways to Put Your Life in Order

Sweet Publishing
Ft. Worth, Texas
G.R. Welch Ltd., Canada

Unless otherwise noted, scripture quotations are from the *Holy Bible: New International Version* (NIV), copyright © 1978 by the International Bible Society. Used by permission of Zondervan Bible Publishers.

MAKING THINGS RIGHT, *When Things Go Wrong*

Ten Proven Ways to Put Your Life in Order

3934 Sandshell, Fort Worth, Texas 76137-2403

Library of Congress Card Catalog Number 86-061405

ISBN 0-8344-0137-1

 10 9 8 7 6 5 4 3 2 1

Dedication

This book is dedicated to my mother and father. Dad, the quiet, gentle, patient man in my life. One whom I never heard utter an unkind or hostile word — truly a rarity in today's world. But Dad has been gone from this world several years now. I'll have to wait a while longer to get better acquainted with him.

Mom is going on 92. She provided the spunk, the zap and the thunder in our house at 1000 Washington Street (long since torn down). She also filled the house with music and parties (a la fudge, popcorn balls and, best of all, the most wonderful taffy west of the Mississippi). She was, and still is, an avid reader and an inspiration to all who know her. This is for you, Mother.

Your son,

Paul

Preface

This book assumes that if anything *can*
go wrong, it *will* . . .
not so much because of Murphy's Law,
but because of Satan's influence.

It further assumes that nothing
can go wrong that Christ
can't make right.

"We are more than conquerors through him"
(Romans 8:37).

Acknowledgements

All writers have help, and this book is no exception. I want to thank Sweet Publishing, especially its president, Byron Williamson, for the push and encouragement. Also thanks to the staff at Sweet Publishing, especially Mary Hollingsworth for unbelieveable rewrite and editing chores.

I am also grateful to Harry Gipson who worked with me as a research editor in the development of the material in book form.

Most of all, thanks to Gladys, my wife, who has listened to me present this material in its various birthing forms for the past three years all over the country and some foreign countries. Her assessment didn't stop with verbal feedback, as the staff at Sweet knows. She had a big part in writing and editing the material as well. Thanks again, Honey.

Paul

Dr. Paul Faulkner
P. O. Box 7518
Abilene, TX 79699

Contents

Introduction

Things go wrong in life. That's all there is to it. And when they do, you must choose how to react. *Making Things Right, When Things Go Wrong* is a practical Christian discussion of how to straighten out tangled-up life situations, written in Dr. Faulkner's comfortable language that nobody can misunderstand.

Based on university studies related to "Functional and Dysfunctional Marriages," as well as other professional psychological research, Faulkner explains ten proven ways to put your life in order. This book is the culmination of more than four years' research and development by Dr. Faulkner.

Due to the popularity of Dr. Faulkner's seminars and the highly successful *Marriage Enrichment* film series which he co-authored, New Day Productions has produced a series of five films by the same title as this book. These films focus on five of the ten techniques discussed: Choose a Positive Disposition; Act Better Than You Feel; Cut Your Line When It's Tangled; Keep Cool, Even When You're Hot and Make Your Relationships Right. This film series is available through your local Christian Film Library or by contacting New Day Productions tollfree at 1-800-531-5220 (outside Texas) or 1-800-252-9213 (in Texas).

It is hoped by Dr. Faulkner and the publisher that *Making Things Right, When Things Go Wrong* will be a practical reference guide and an inspirational help to its readers. It is founded on the principle that a right relationship with God will enable you to successfully untangle life's knottiest problems. And it is hoped that God himself will receive the glory for any workable ideas you may find in this book.

Attitudes are more important than facts.

— Karl Menninger

It's up to you to change your life. It's up to you to make things right when things go wrong. And God has given you the power to do it.

CHAPTER ONE

Choose a Positive Disposition

A fellow named George owned an apartment complex and had just completed the exterior brick work on the second floor. He had some bricks left over and was trying to decide the best way to get the load of bricks back down to ground level without breaking them. He noticed a 55-gallon barrel on the ground and thought, "I know what I'll do. I'll tie some rope around that barrel, hook a pulley to the second-floor eave and pull the barrel up to the second floor. Then I can load the bricks into the barrel and let it back down to the ground."

So, that's what he began to do. He tied the rope around the barrel, ran it over the pulley on the second floor and pulled the barrel up to second-story level. Then he tied the rope to the root of a nearby tree. He went up to the second floor balcony and loaded the bricks into the barrel. Then he went back downstairs, grabbed the rope and pulled it loose from the root.

Now, folks, that 55-gallon drum full of bricks was four times heavier than George. So the barrel shot down lickety split, and George shot up lickety split. And you *know* what happened. As George shot past the barrel, it hit his shoulder, slammed against his hip and whomped his kneecap. The barrel crashed to the ground, and George's head smashed into the pulley above, cracking his skull. There he was, dangling by the rope from the second-story roof.

When the barrel hit the ground, the bricks were so heavy they knocked the bottom out of the barrel. So, now George was heavier than the barrel. Yep! Down he went, and up it came. This time, the barrel caught him on the other side. It whomped his other knee, scraped past his other hip, broke his nose and dumped him on top of the pile of leftover bricks below. He turned both ankles, scuffed up his shins, and the corners of the bricks punched him in the side. So George let out a yell and turned loose of the rope.

You guessed it. Now the barrel was four times heavier than the rope, so it came bombing down on top of George to finish the job from the previous hit-and-run. And George found himself lying in the hospital, bruised, sprained and broken, saying to himself, "I don't know whether to file one insurance claim or five."

A MIXED-UP PLACE

We are living in a world of "ubiquitous ambivalence" (forever going back and forth—up and down). Our balance is always being tested. About the time you have your bucket filled, the bottom falls out. Just when you get into your favorite TV program, the phone rings. These things happen with such regularity that you must accept the fact that this is normal. To expect life to flow smoothly with few bumps is abnormal.

I think most of us sometimes feel like George. Life has dumped us bruised, sprained and broken on its pile of leftovers. We're all whomped up and don't think we can even get up and walk away. That's just the nature of the way things happen in this life. Things do go wrong. Everything is always up in the air, at least here on earth!

So how are you going to make things right in this old world of ubiquitous ambivalence? (Those big words just basically mean the world's a mixed-up place.) There's good, there's bad, there are all kinds of problems in life. It doesn't come to you straight — it comes all mixed up. You have to straighten it out for yourself. But how? Where do you start?

ATTITUDE ADJUSTMENT

If you want to make wrong things right, if you want to set the world straight, if you want to get your act together, you have to get your attitude right. Get your heart right. Everything you are and do are products of your attitude about life.

All of God's creatures lug around an atmosphere, wherever they go. When a little black-and-white bundle of fuzz called a skunk is around, he's in full charge of the atmosphere — both his and yours. The skunk has no choice. But if your attitude stinks and is fouling up the atmosphere for those around you, it's because you choose to stink. When *your* attitudes go wrong, you can choose to make them right.

Your disposition sets you apart, in one way or another — a positive way or a negative way. Do people stay away from you as they would a skunk? Or are people attracted to you as they are to a single bright star in the night? "Do all things without grumbling or arguing so that you may become blameless and pure — in a crooked generation in which you shine like stars in the universe as you hold out the word of life" (Philippians 2:14).

Right attitudes are the foundation stones of successful living. All that you are and do today is the sum total of your thoughts and attitudes of yesterday. You will travel the path tomorrow which your heart and mind blaze today. The thoughts, images and perceptions cast upon the screens of your mind become the blueprints you will use to build your future.

The Bible says, "As a man thinketh in his heart, so is he" (Proverbs 23:7, *KJV*). It adds, "Above all else, guard your heart, for it is the wellspring of life" (Proverbs 4:23).

Do you hear what the Bible is saying to you? Peter looked at Simon the magician and said, "You've got heart problems" (Acts 8:21). Jesus looked at the people of Jerusalem and said, "Their hearts are far from me" (Matthew 15:8). Heart problems can mess up your life.

Karl Menninger, a celebrated psychiatrist, said, "Attitudes are more important than facts." But we humans have always had a tendency to judge a person by his outward appearance (facts). This happened when Samuel saw Eliab and thought God would surely anoint him king. Eliab was good-looking, tall, seemingly a fine man. But God said: "Do not consider his appearance or his height, for I have rejected him. The Lord does not look at the things man looks at. Man looks at the outward appearance, but the Lord looks at the heart" (1 Samuel 16:6-7).

You can always spot folks with bad attitudes. They swell up like a toad when they don't get their way. They're always grumpy and out of sorts. Read this out loud to yourself: "Murmur, murmur, murmur." Sounds just like what it means, doesn't it? God said the Israelites were murmuring and complaining. Can't you just hear them? Or there's the boy murmuring as he walks through the garage into the yard after you have told him to mow the grass. Can't you hear him? As I was growing up, my mother would sometimes tell me, "Paul, you just have a bad attitude." And you have probably heard the response loud and clear: "I do *not*!" I gave myself away with that answer.

I heard about one fella who said to his complaining friend, "Did you wake up grumpy this morning?"

And the friend replied, "No, I just let her sleep." He couldn't see his own grumpy attitude, but he could sure see it in someone else. And that's typical, isn't it?

ARE YOU OUT OF SYNC?

A biblical character that touches me is David. He touches me because I see myself so plainly in him—a fellow who messes up. He made so many mistakes and, yet, the Bible says, ". . . he was a man after God's own heart" (1 Samuel 13:14). And, oh how I hope that I can just have his heart. David's attitude of heart is obvious in Psalm 51. It just twists your heart and breaks it. That's what God wants to do, you know. He wants to break your heart. He wants to get right down there with you and adjust your attitude.

David says, "God, against you, you only, have I sinned" (Psalm 51:4). Well, David, didn't you sin against this man when you killed him? Didn't you sin against this woman, Bathsheba? But, you see, David hit it right at the core of the problem. If you never sin against God, you don't have to worry about your fellowman.

The "big" sin is against God. If you get right with God, and your heart's right with him, you don't have to worry about having a problem with other people; it will take care of itself.

And that's where I find myself and you probably find yourself. Is your heart right with God? If so, you are likely right with your family, friends and co-workers, too. If your attitudes rebel against God, you're likely "out of sync" with those around you as well. It's a direct parallel.

PREDISPOSITION

Do you ever decide before you even meet a person that you're not going to like him? Do you ever make up your mind before you go to church: "I'm not going to like it"? Or before you go to the company picnic, do you think, "It will be boring"? The fact is you usually find exactly what you expect to find. Your predispositions determine beforehand the way you will see things.

Consider the perceptions of two neighbors: The first husband wakes up in the morning and looks at his wife. Her hair is in rollers. Her face is covered with cold cream. There's a rip in her robe. The guy thinks: "Man, what on earth am I doing hooked up with this?"

The fellow next door wakes up in the morning, looks at his wife and sees the same things. Her hair is in rollers. Her face is covered with cold cream. There's a rip in her robe. But he thinks: "Isn't she a doll? She jumps up in the morning, fixes breakfast and gets the kids off to school before she takes care of herself! What a doll!"

What made the difference? Attitude! Psychological tests reveal that our responses toward others are determined more by our attitudes than by what others actually do. It's all in how we look at things.

For example, a child spills a glass of milk. Mama is in a good mood, so she says, "Oh, dear, the milk is spilled. I'll make a dam with this napkin. You run get a towel, and we'll clean it up." When her disposition is cheerful, the mother addresses the *issue*, which is the milk, not the child.

Two weeks later, the same child spills some milk and the same mom points her finger at the horror-struck child and shouts, "If I've told you once, I've told you a thousand times not to set your milk so close to the edge of the table!(and then there is the usual hook) Haven't I? Haven't I?" The mother makes what the child *does* the issue, not the milk. Do you remember being at the end of one of those pointing fingers? You don't know whether to shake, cry or just roll over and play dead.

How do you treat someone when they mess up? Do you put them down with a hook like, "I've told you a thousand times, haven't I?" Do you kick them while they're down? Or do you gently pick them up, dust them off and get them going again? It all depends on whether you are predisposed to find the negative or the positive in life and people. You'll find what you're looking for every time.

Seeing the Possibilities

It's night on the Sea of Galilee. Jesus' disciples look up, rowing hard. Things are pretty rough in the boat because the sea is tossing about from the winds and raging storm. Then they see a ghost, they think, walking calmly toward them across the pitching water. They are wet and cold and scared. In fact, they're frightened to death.

Then the Lord says to them, "Don't be afraid; it is I."

Peter responds immediately, saying, "Lord, if it's really you, tell me to come to you on the water." I figure there's a bit of a question in Peter's tone here. As usual, he may have blurted out the question without really thinking about what he was saying. And Jesus, who is always predisposed to see the possibilities for others, says, "Come on."

Now what are you going to do if you're Peter? Bless his heart, Peter just steps out and begins to walk on the water. He walks all the way to Jesus, however far that was. The Bible doesn't tell us how far he walked. He's the only human being that ever walked on water, but what do we remember about the story? We just remember the negative. Foomp! Down he goes. Peter took his eyes off Jesus! He stopped to survey the problems that made his walk on water logically impossible. Peter doubted. Peter failed. Peter sank.

Now here's Peter treading water, wet as can be, and crying out, "Lord, save me!" What does Jesus say? Well, we don't know. We're just going to have to wait for the big replay to know that, but I'm going to guess. I'm going to guess that he *didn't* say, "If I've told you once, I've told you a thousand times, haven't I?" I'm going to guess that he said, "Peter, isn't it amazing what you can do when you keep your eyes on me?"

LOOKING ON THE BRIGHT SIDE

Let's look at Peter's efforts again, this time from a positive mind-set as Jesus would. Peter did walk on water! No one on earth ever walked further on water than Peter did. No one, that is, but Jesus. His name ought to be in the *Guinness Book of World Records* under the heading: Water-walking. By Jesus' power, Peter actually accomplished the impossible. We usually forget Peter's achievement because we are prone to focus on the negative. Let's give him credit and focus on the positive.

It seems that every time Peter failed and was ready to give up on himself, he expected Jesus to give up on him, too. But Jesus always stayed with him in his moments of failure. Peter always found himself looking up into positive eyes that loved him and simply would not give up on him. Through every failure, every disappointment, it was Jesus' steadfast love for him that prompted Peter to get up and try again and again. Jesus' attitude was (and *is*) contagious.

If each of us looked at everybody with the eyes of a love that never gave up, ugly attitudes would never whittle anybody down to "their proper size."

A POWERFUL PREDISPOSITION

Do you remember the story of the Syro-Phoenician woman in Mark 7:24-30? She came to Jesus about her daughter. You know how mothers are about their children. They never give up.

She said to Jesus: "I've got a daughter possessed with a demon." Unlike the Jesus we know, he gave her the silent treatment. Have you ever gotten the silent treatment? How does it make you feel? But she doesn't let this stop her. She keeps talking. "Lord, help me."

The disciples surrounding Jesus say: "Lord, would you send this woman away? She keeps buggin' us." They've insulted her, but she keeps coming back, asking for help.

Jesus says: "Woman, I wasn't sent to you. I was sent to the lost sheep of the house of Israel. Not to you heathens."

What a put-down! But what's her attitude? It's still pleasant and determined. "Lord, please help me."

You won't believe what Jesus said at this fourth interaction. "Woman, you don't take the food for the children and give it to the dogs."

You say, "He wouldn't say that!" But he did! Well, why did he say it? That's four put-downs, and the last time he calls her a dog. Yes, but wonder and glory at her response.

She said, "Even the dogs get the crumbs. Just give me a crumb, Lord." It's enough! What a fantastic attitude!

Now don't you ever try that with anyone. You may get into trouble. But Jesus knew her heart; he knew how far he could take her and test her and that her disposition would still stay beautiful. He wanted to bring out her fantastic attitude as an example for us all. How is your attitude when you are up against put-downs and discouraging circumstances?

Negative attitudes toward people and things distort our mental capacity to see things as they really are. So, we respond foolishly or irrationally to the bogus notions our minds invent about people and events.

Most of us can identify with the little boy who was afraid of the dark because of the frightening things he kept making up in his head. His mother encouraged him to go out into the dark to conquer his irrational fears.

"Walk on out into the dark," she urged. "You'll be all right. God is out there, and he will take care of you."

Gathering courage, the boy walked out the door, took a few steps and stopped. Peering out into the darkness he said, "Okay, God, if you're really out there, don't move a muscle or you'll scare me to death!"

I could have been that boy. I've been scared at night by monsters and men ten feet tall who were coming to get me. I often saw what I believed was there.

TWO BASIC ATTITUDES

In Luke 15, Jesus tells a story of two sons who went wrong because of their bad attitudes. One of them messed up his life *away* from his father's house—a "dumb" sinner. The other messed up his life *in* the father's house — a "smart" sinner.

"There was a man who had two sons." (The man in the parable represents God.) The younger of the sons said, "Father, give me my share of the estate." The boy wanted to be free! Living at home meant parental control. He wanted to shake that. He wanted to go to the breakfast table without having to answer probing questions: "Where did you go last night?" "What did you do?" "Who were you with?" "What time did you get in?" Father's rules! Well, spit on Father's rules! He wanted to be free. He'd make the decisions. He'd call the shots.

The father could have said, "Son, I don't like your attitude" and then refused his son's demand. But had he refused to give the boy his share of the property, it would only have made his son hostile. So he gave him the freedom to go wrong, praying that the painful experience he knew was coming would prompt the son someday to make things right again.

So the boy was released from the restraints of his father's house. He took his share of the family wealth and traveled "into a distant country."

FOLLOWING YOUR HEART

You realize that his adventure into partyland, a paradise of loose and immoral living, was no spur-of-the-moment affair. It was predetermined. The "want to" was planted in his mind long before the dust of the distant country was on his feet. "Where your heart is, your feet will follow."

It wasn't a *storm* with a demanding father that propelled the feet of the prodigal toward the distant country. It was the set of his heart and mind that pulled them there. It was his attitude.

God says to man, "My thoughts are not your thoughts; neither are my ways your ways" (Isaiah 55:8).

Let's face it. All the problems of mankind arise because we want to "do *our* thing" instead of God's. I am my own number one problem. I am responsible for my choices and accountable for my actions.

As the young prodigal's sandals pounded their way to the faraway country, he was as happy as a hen pouncing on a june bug. He fantasized about the loose and immoral climate. There he could live on his own terms, be his own boss and not have to answer to anyone. He was free!

Or was he? Soon he would discover that absolute freedom is like those men and monsters who are ten feet tall that come in the dark to grab you . . . an illusion. And we are never as free as when we willingly submit our attitudes and actions to the rules and regulations of our loving and compassionate Father in heaven. There is real freedom! All other freedom is only an illusion. This is why we call the young son a "dumb" sinner—the pay off is too costly. It's not even a *smart* choice, much less a *right* choice.

TURNING THINGS AROUND

Look closely at what happened to the boy after he went stone broke in the distant country. "He went and hired himself out to a citizen of that country, who sent him into his fields to feed pigs." Note that the boy wasn't asked if he *wanted* to go feed pigs. He had no choice. He was *sent*. Now he finds himself in a prison erected by his own selfish attitude.

There he sits in the pigpen, his self-esteem squandered. He's broke. Friendless. Starving. He tries to ease his hunger by eating the husks the pigs couldn't. Remember now, this is the boy who wanted his freedom and independence. This is the fellow who was going to satisfy every sensual urge of his flesh, and now he is dying of starvation. He is in desperate need of a changed attitude about life.

Here's the key: not only can we change our attitudes, we can change them in any set of circumstances. Think about the thief on the cross, for instance. He was nailed to a cross, in excruciating pain. It was a horrible circumstance, to say the least. He had apparently been railing away at Jesus; then he had a change of heart, a change of mind. He changed his attitude from bad to good in the midst of the most horrible circumstances. You can change your attitude, your mind set, your heart, in *any* set of circumstances.

Ella Wheeler Wilcox wrote this truth in poetry:

> One ship sails east and another west
> while the self-same breezes blow.
> 'Tis the set of the sail and not the gale
> that bids them where they go.
>
> As the winds of the air are the ways of fate
> as we voyage along through life.
> 'Tis the set of the soul that decides our goal
> and not the storm and the strife.

The apostle Paul said it this way: "I have learned to be content whatever the circumstances" (Philippians 4:11). And that was a mouthful for a guy who was beaten, put in prison, stoned, shipwrecked and chased out of town after town. Yet, do you find it difficult to be content even in the lap of luxury? Attitude—that's the difference.

FACING COLD, HARD REALITY

It's significant that the prodigal began to change at the precise moment that he changed his attitude and began to see things as they actually were. He came to his senses as the truth seeped into his heart: "My Father isn't responsible for the actions which have led to my misery. I am the culprit. I am responsible. Therefore, I will change. I will set out and go back to my father and say to him, 'Father, I have sinned.'" And in his wonderful victory over pride, he decided to go home, confess his sin and ask his father to put him on the payroll as a common servant.

Some folks might think the young prodigal was just *conning* his father, to get dad to feel sorry for him. The truth is, the young man's heart was broken, just like David's. He was not only willing to go back and serve God as a hired servant, but it also meant serving under his older, record-keeping brother. That was all right. Now that his heart had been broken, he could serve others with no resentment. He was just thankful to have a job with a loving father.

Of course, it didn't work out that way. With open arms, his father welcomed home a penitent and broken-hearted son. His father covered him with royal apparel — a robe on his shoulders, a ring on his finger and shoes on his feet. He killed the fatted calf for a banquet feast and called in all of his friends and neighbors to celebrate the return of his son. In the banquet hall everyone was rejoicing with the father over the return of a wayward boy whose attitude had drastically changed.

The older son was out in the field. His father sent a servant out to invite him to come to the banquet feast and celebrate the return of his only brother. "But he became angry and refused to go in." He stood outside hearing the music, sulking about the fuss being made over the return of his forgiven brother and resenting the happiness that was in his father's heart.

Have you ever been around someone who turns down your invitations or pouts if they can't be the center of attention? They create diversions or do anything they can to rain on your parade and dampen others' happiness.

Have you ever known people who stick out their bottom lips and pout with resentful, jealous attitudes? Some people, like the older brother, think they are too good to need forgiveness and that ordinary sinners, like most of us, don't deserve it.

ANALYZING YOUR GRIPES

It's amazing how much you can learn about a person, just by listening to his list of gripes. Let's see what we can learn about the older brother as he bad-mouths his father.

Gripe #1. "Look how many years I have served you."

Attitude. I've worked like a slave for you for a long, long time. But do you appreciate anything I've ever done? No way!

Observations. He resents his father for not giving him preferential treatment for services rendered. He feels his father is unjust and unfair in his attitudes toward him. But had he not been graciously born into this family, he would have nothing.

Gripe #2. "I have never broken your rules; I always obeyed you."

Attitude. I'm your good son, not your bad one. My younger brother left you in a lurch, but I have never wronged you!

Observation. He has obeyed his father all right, but with a selfish ulterior motive — the "smart" sinner. Because he has never wronged his father, he feels he has the right to hate and resent a brother who has wronged his father.

Gripe #3. "And yet, you never gave me even a kid that I might celebrate with my friends."

Attitude. You've never rewarded me for being such an obedient and dutiful son. How do I know? Because you've never given me even a little goat so that I could celebrate with my friends. If only you had held a little barbeque-picnic in my honor and told my friends how much you appreciate me, I would have been happy.

Observation. Just a little goat meat and a few kind words would have made him happy. Who is he kidding? With his attitude, he'll never be happy.

Gripe #4. "But when this son of *yours* comes. . . ."

Attitude. He's not my brother, Father. He's your son. I don't recognize him as a brother, and I refuse to treat him as one.

Observation. He is totally self-centered. *I* serve. *I* obey. *I* do no wrong. You make no fuss over *me*. You never gave *me* a kid. As dutiful as he was, he had no love in his heart for his brother. The one thing the older son lacked was the thing he most needed. For, "How can we love God whom we have not seen, if we don't love our brother whom we have seen" (John 4:20)?

What the older son failed to realize was that his loveless attitudes and selfish disposition were no less sinful in the eyes of his father than the outward rebellion and immoral acts of his younger brother. By refusing to go in to the feast where everyone could rejoice together, he slammed the door to joy in his own face.

All who go to enjoy that feast must have at least this one thing in common: "By *this* all men will know that you are my disciples, if you love one another" (John 13:35).

Heart Trouble

Is he us? The older son illustrates the kind of ungracious, unattractive goodness of some religious folks today. True, he stayed at home in his father's house. He sowed no wild oats, wasted no money nor scarred his soul with loose, riotous living — all of which are in his favor. But this older brother was a loveless, selfish and fault-finding sourpuss. He can't get along with his father, and he can't get along with others. It's a negative mind-set — an attitude and heart problem.

THOSE UGLY RASCALS

Bad attitudes breed some ugly rascals in your life that go around offending, insulting and alienating nearly everybody. More often than not, it's your "gottas" that get you.

Mr. Gotta-Win

The first ugly rascal is Mr. Gotta-Win. You've gotta win this game, that contract, that position. Whatever the cost, you've gotta win it. America has good soil and climate for the gottas. You want to be the top dog or nothing at all. If you can't win, you won't play. If you lose, you complain and let them know you'll leave cleat-marks on their faces the next time. One problem created by a win-at-all-cost attitude is that the moment you become the top dog, everyone around you rallies to the aid of the next underdog. Why? They just don't like your attitude. Your gotta-win attitude has gotta lose.

I've had to wrestle with this one. I can't even sit down and play dominoes or a tiddlywinks without the gotta-win attitude getting me. Somehow, you've got to develop an attitude that plays the game for the game's sake and doesn't want to embarrass others. That's tough. But it's a price you should be willing to pay in order to keep things right with others.

Mr. Gotta-Be-Consulted

The second ugly rascal is Mr. Gotta-Be-Consulted. Before any plans or decisions are made, I gotta be consulted. And if I am not consulted, I go off somewhere to sulk and pout. "What's wrong with you?" you ask. "Well, he didn't check with me first." Or, "He couldn't have cared less about what *I* wanted." Is that you?

Mr. Gotta-Be-Seen

A third ugly rascal is Mr. Gotta-Be-Seen. I've gotta get in the front of the group so when they snap the picture I'll be seen. I've gotta sit at the head of the table so everyone will notice me.

The valet of the last German Kaiser had this appraisal of him: "I cannot deny that my master was vain. He had to be the central figure in everything. If he went to a christening, he wanted to be the baby; if he went to a wedding, he wanted to be the bride; if he went to a funeral, he wanted to be the corpse."

Why have we gotta win and gotta be consulted and gotta be seen? We give in to our "gottas" to give our egos a temporary boost from the low opinion we generally have of ourselves. If I can win over others, if others will consult me, if others can see me, then they will love me and appreciate me. But it doesn't work out that way, does it? Instead, the gottas get you. The very principles that we practice to cause others to respect us are the same ones that destroy our relationships with those whom we are trying to impress. Taking these attitudes into your marriage, your home, your business and the church will cause relationships to go wrong.

WHEN THINGS GO WRONG

Things are going to go wrong in your life. That's the way life is. It's a series of mishaps and problems that you must solve. It's like a mouse trying to run a maze. There's a place to go in and a place to come out, but there are a lot of dead-ends and walls to overcome in between. When you hit a wall, you just have to change your attitude, your heart and your action to make them right. If you don't change your direction, you just keep butting your head against the wall, because the wall won't budge.

It's up to *you* to change your life. It's up to *you* to make things right when things go wrong. And God has given you the power to do it. "I can do everything through him who gives me strength" (Philippians 4:13).

Grab your "wanter" by your "willer" and make yourself do what you know you ought to do, and God will help you do it.

I have learned the secret of being content in any and every situation.
— Philippians 4:11

CHAPTER TWO

Will To, Whether You Want To or Not

Robert was physically handicapped. He was a spastic and confined to a wheelchair because his muscle movements could not be controlled. Robert's speech was so slurred that he was difficult to understand. You're probably thinking: "Poor guy. What a miserable life." But, wait!

Robert was a student in the university where I taught. And what a delightful person he was. He was a favorite among the students because his attitude was so wonderful. He had his *willer* in control and was living a full and exciting life.

Robert couldn't write, so he would carry carbon paper with him to class and ask the student next to him to put the carbon paper under his own paper as he took notes. If that student took good notes, Robert had good notes. If not, Robert had poor notes, too.

He couldn't pull himself forward in his wheelchair, so if no one was around to push him, Robert just turned around and pushed himself backward with his feet, looking over his shoulder to see where he was going.

One day Robert came too close to the edge of some stairs in the administration building. Robert, wheelchair, books and all went tumbling and crashing down the stairs. The wheelchair rolled off down the hall, and Robert ended up sprawled out on the floor but relatively unhurt. Several concerned students rushed over to help him. From his rather undignified position, Robert looked up at his rescuers, laughed out loud and said, "Let me teach you how to dance!"

Robert wanted to preach and share the message of Christ with others. One Sunday he spoke to a large crowd of over a thousand Christians in church. He sat in his wheelchair on the podium with his Bible in his lap. He struggled hard to speak plainly and to not let his arms wave about. Very few people in that audience understood all of Robert's actual words that day, but not one person missed the message of the love of God he communicated. There wasn't a dry eye in the place when he finished. And everyone went away trying to remember what their own flimsy excuses were that kept them from sharing God's love with others. How legitimate it would have been for Robert to make the same excuse Moses made: "Lord, I just don't speak well enough." But he didn't.

The last time I heard about Robert he had gone with a group of missionaries overseas. He had them put posters on the sides of his wheelchair and park him on a busy downtown street corner. There he sat all day every day handing out tracts to passers-by about the Lord that was so important to him. He truly had the mind of Christ. And he had, indeed, become the dynamic preacher he so *wanted* and *willed* himself to be.

See, folks, Robert had learned to be content in his seemingly impossible circumstances. He was making the most of what he *had* and not worrying about what he *didn't have.* He had mastered his circumstances with his good attitude, instead of allowing his circumstances to master him.

GET A HANDLE ON YOUR "WANTER"

The only way to make things right when things go wrong is usually the last thing you want to do. You have to *want* to turn your thoughts, attitudes and actions over to the Specialist who, by the way, has never yet been handed a case he couldn't handle. You have to say, "Father, I *want* to make your thoughts my thoughts and your ways my ways." You have to get a handle on your "wanter."

Good news! "We can choose our attitude in any set of circumstances," says Lord Byron. And that's true. Circumstances — either favorable or unfavorable — just don't count when you really *want* to change your attitude and actions.

William James, the noted Harvard psychologist, said, "The greatest discovery in our generation [and that's a lot of territory] is that human beings by changing the inner attitudes of their minds can change all the outer aspects of their lives." If he's right, by changing your attitudes you can be liberated from those things in your life that are preventing your living in a happy, meaningful way. And he *is* right! It's hopefully, encouragingly and wonderfully true! You can change your attitude and make many of your most challenging dreams a present reality.

LIVING RIGHT IN AN ALL-WRONG WORLD

What's needed is an inner attitude, an unshakable conviction that, regardless of the circumstances which life may send your way, with God's help you can triumph *in* your troubles, if not *over* them. To triumph in your troubles is really the only victory you need, ". . . because great is your reward in heaven" (Matthew 5:12).

That affirming attitude reminds me of Viktor Frankl, a bold and courageous Jewish psychiatrist who was arrested by the Nazis and imprisoned in Auschwitz during the World War II holocaust. Standing almost naked in a cold prison courtyard, the victim of undeserved cruelty at the hands of his enemies, Frankl lifted his eyes to a tall smokestack. He saw the cremated bodies of friends and loved ones being discharged into the atmosphere as smoke and ashes. Looking around him, he saw prisoners who were willing to fight over a little piece of string they could use to wrap their feet. He saw some of them choosing to throw away their lives on an electric fence surrounding the prison, rather than to continue their miserable existence.

In those dispirited times, Frankl observed that the one thing most needed by despairing men was a change of attitude. He said:

> We had to learn ourselves and, furthermore, we had to teach the despairing men that it really didn't matter what was expected of life, but rather what life expected of us. We needed to stop asking about the meaning of life, but instead think of ourselves as those who were being questioned by life daily, hourly. Our answer must consist not in talk or meditation, but in right action and conduct. Life ultimately means taking the responsibility to find the right answer to its problems, and to fulfill the task which is constantly set for each individual.

Frankl also said, "The last great human freedom is the ability to choose one's attitude in any given circumstance."

Learn to Be Content

In the first century, long before psychiatry became a reality, the apostle Paul demonstrated this principle. Here's what he wrote to his brethren in the city of Philippi: ". . . I have learned to be content whatever the circumstances" (Philippians 4:11). And Paul had been in some miserable circumstances. On one occasion he was falsely accused, beaten and thrown into prison where he was shackeled hand and foot. He was put in the inner prison (which we'd call the maximum security cell). But at midnight, of all things, Paul was singing. And he wasn't wailing the words to "Nobody Knows the Trouble I've Seen" either. He was singing *praises* to God (see Acts 16:25)! What a fantastic attitude in such dire circumstances. But if your heart is right with God, circumstances just don't count. Now, that may not sound very revolutionary the first time you hear it, but the idea grows on you. It suggests a truth that everyone has to wrestle with sooner or later: Until you're able to be happy in *every* situation, you can't really be happy in *any* situation.

No matter how hard you try to convince yourself to the contrary, your happiness and satisfaction in life are not determined by your actual circumstances but by your attitude toward those circumstances. If you can just learn the secret of being content in any situation, that in itself will make life a very meaningful and significant affair.

HOW DO YOU CHANGE YOUR ATTITUDES?

How can you learn to be content in any situation? How can you achieve this significant goal in life?

Believe You Can

The answer is simple: Believe you can. Some psychologists would say that you can find happiness and contentment in life through your own human resources. They view each person as a self-sufficient being who can manufacture his own do-it-yourself kit to achieve whatever he believes. But I question that philosophy. I know many self-sufficient folks who see no need for an enabling power above or beyond their own. Yet, I know very few who have learned to be content "whatever the circumstances." God has made it clear that whatever we accomplish is not by our own power, "but by my Spirit, says the Lord Almighty" (Zechariah 4:2).

How did Paul learn to be content in any set of circumstances? Did he learn it through his own human self-sufficiency? No way! Rather, he said, "I have learned the secret of being content in any and every situation . . . I can do all things *through him* [Christ] who strengthens me" (Philippians 4:11-13). These are among the most familiar words in the New Testament, but I'm not sure we really understand their significance.

What exactly did Paul mean by this stunning claim? Was he actually saying that with Christ's help he could do *anything*? Some folks take it that way, but does that fit the context of what Paul said? I don't think Paul is claiming to be some sort of superman who can pray for Christ's help and then leap buildings in a single bound or catch bullets in his teeth. He is simply saying what any committed Christian can say: "In Christ's strength I can be content in whatever circumstances life may choose to hurl at me. His Spirit will help me do anything God wants me to do. Paul learned the secret of contentment because he believed that with Christ's help he could learn to be content in any situation. And that power is available to you, too. But you have to *believe* you can!

Role Models

Another good role model to follow in learning contentment is the prophet Habakkuk, who could say:

> Though the fig tree does not bud, and there are no grapes on the vines, though the olive crop fails and the fields produce no food, though there are no sheep in the pen and no cattle in the stalls; yet, I will rejoice in the Lord, I will be joyful in God my Savior (Habakkuk 3:17-18).

These are certainly not the words of a man who allows negative circumstances in life to spoil his personal happiness. If we could translate Habakkuk's words into idioms of today, it might run something like this:

> Though I'm living in a general recession, and my income has plummeted to zero; though I've lost my job, and my unemployment benefits expired yesterday; though I'm hungry, out of groceries and don't know where my next meal is coming from; still I will rejoice in the Lord, I find joy in my Savior.

One Christian who found great strength in the Lord, despite much personal suffering, was Edith Euss, a young wife and mother who died of lupus at age 34. Before her death she wrote:

> Joy is knowing that even our crosses in life can be used by God for his glory and our good. We are too finite to see the overall picture, but we can trustingly thank him even for the pain, because we have the assurance that though he doesn't deliberately cause us pain, he is still there and in control. Joy is this reassurance, but it is also more. Joy is a deep, soul-realizing knowledge that whatever our situation, God is hanging in there with us. He rejoices when we rejoice; he cries when we cry. He allows us our free will, even though he knows we will hurt ourselves by it, just because he loves us so much. He is always there. Emmanuel, God with us. As far as I know, this is the ultimate joy. It is something that death and depression, doubt and lupus flares cannot weaken. Is there even more joy than this? I wonder and thrill at the possibilities.

Contentment, even in the face of death. It is the art of looking at what you have left, rather than what you've lost. It's looking at the donut and not the hole. It's seeing a glass of water as half full, not half empty. It's accentuating the positive and eliminating the negative from your life.

It's a thought worth repeating: The way to change your attitude is to believe through Christ that you can.

Drastic Changes

Dr. Frankl, while a prisoner of the German Gestapo, writes of his acquaintance with the notorious Dr. J, commonly referred to as "the mass murderer of Steinhoff." Steinhoff was a mental hospital in Vienna, Austria. When patients were admitted to the hospital, Dr. J promptly murdered as many of them as he could get his hands on. He delighted in it. Frankl said, "He was the only person I ever met that was truly a Mephistophelian." Do you remember Mephistopheles? He was one of the seven chief devils of medieval demonology. He was the one represented in Goethe's *Faust* as a crafty, sardonic and scoffing fiend. "And that," says Frankl, "describes Dr. J. He was a Satanic individual."

Several years after the war was over, Dr. Frankl discovered that Dr. J had been arrested by the Russians and had died of cancer in a Russian prison camp at the age of 40. The man from whom Frankl learned this news had been a fellow prisoner with Dr. J in the Russian camp.

When Dr. Frankl informed the man of his horrible recollections of the sadistic Dr. J, the man responded, "I don't remember Dr. J as being that way at all when I was imprisoned with him in Russia. Before he died, he showed himself to be the best comrade you can imagine! He gave consolation to everybody. He lived up to the highest conceivable moral standards. He was the best friend I ever met during my long years in prison!" If Dr. J could make such a drastic change, shouldn't you be able to change, too?

A concerned father brought his demon-possessed boy to Jesus to be healed. The Bible says, "When the spirit saw Jesus, it immediately threw the boy into a convulsion. He fell to the ground and rolled around, foaming at the mouth.

"Jesus asked the boy's father, 'How long has he been like this?'

"'From childhood,' the father answered. 'It has often thrown him into fire or water to kill him. But if you can do anything, take pity on us and help us.'

"'If you can?' said Jesus. 'Everything is possible for him who believes'" (Mark 9:20-23).

Do you hear what Jesus said to the man? "What do you mean asking *if I can* do anything to help you! You're talking to one who has limitless power. You're asking the wrong question. It's not *if you can*; it's do you *believe* I can?"

The homosexual community has continually tried to convince themselves and others that they are not responsible for their actions — that they were simply born the way they are. Homosexuals often say to me in therapy, "I can't help it. That's just the way I am." God must be weary of all this rationalization. It's simply not true. Anyone can change, if they believe they can! The Bible tells of many who did. And research is more and more validating that the homosexual can change his lifestyle by changing his attitude and thinking. Naturally, this is true of folks with any kind of emotional or spiritual problem. The first step toward recovery is *believing* you can recover.

Do you remember those hot-tempered brothers called the Sons of Thunder in the Bible? These two guys wanted God to zap the whole population of a Samaritan village with a fireball of destruction because some of its citizens didn't want to give Jesus a place to spend the night. But Jesus helped these two surly, ill-tempered fellows change themselves into servant apostles. Isn't it obvious that he has the power to help you change your life, too? The question is: Do you *believe* he can?

GRAB YOUR WANTER BY YOUR WILLER

Once you *believe* you can change your attitude and learn to be content in any set of circumstances, then you must *decide you will* change. The fact is, you can *will* to change. You can grab your "wanter" by your "willer" and turn your life around! You can will to, whether you want to or not.

Abraham Lincoln once observed that, "People are about as happy as they choose to be." And that's about right, isn't it? Even among non-religious folks there are some who are happier than others. Why? It's because they have come to grips with life in a more responsible manner than others. Their lives are under control because they have their *wanters* in submission to their *willers*.

Even long before Lincoln, the Bible said it: "If anyone *chooses* [wills] to do God's will, he will find out my teaching comes from God . . ." (John 7:17). It's a choice you make! You have to choose to be happy; you have to choose to do God's will; you can choose to change your life. Your *willer* is in control.

An important principle that is repeated often through the Bible runs something like this: "If *you will* to do God's will, *he will* help you do his will." But if you choose *not* to do God's will? Well, he just refuses to work in unsurrendered territory. He will respect your desires. But if *you* will, *he* will.

I like the way Paul says it in Philippians 2:12-13: "Therefore, my dear friends, as you have always obeyed — not only in my presence, but now much more in my absence — continue to work out your salvation with fear and trembling, for it is God who works in you to will and to act according to his good purpose." In other words, when you *will* yourself to obey God and work his will in your life, God works in you and strengthens your will to act according to his good purposes. Changing your attitude and behavior through faith is no snap assignment, but God stands ready to help you through his indwelling and enabling Spirit. You can learn to be content in all circumstances as Paul did. If you *believe* it and *will* it, God will enable you to say, "I can do everything through him who gives me strength" (Philippians 4:13).

Some folks say, "I'm not sure I *want* to will to change." Well, grab your *wanter* by your *willer* and make yourself! Do what you know you ought to do, and God will help you do it. Decide "I'm gonna do it." The prodigal son pointed his feet back toward contentment in his father's home when he changed his attitude. He grabbed his *wanter* (he really wanted to live a life of luxury in partyland) by his *willer* (he knew he needed to go home to his father) and said, "I *will* arise and go to my father" (Luke 15:18). Like Abe said, "You can be about as happy as you choose to be."

Comparison Kills Contentment

Contentment largely depends on your ability to be satisfied with what you have and not worry about what everybody else has. The administration of a small university faced that problem in a decision they were forced to make. The problem? The administration had difficulty employing or keeping qualified professors in the business college at the salary being offered. Those who teach in the business college have to be Certified Public Accountants and have doctorate degrees. The business community was hiring these candidates at twice the salary being offered by the university, and it was tough to compete. So the administration was forced to decide to offer salaries more competitive with the business community in order to retain qualified staff. And they did.

Well, that sounds fine in theory, unless you happen to be a professor in another department that is not receiving the salary boost. Naturally, the inconsistency of salaries set the university faculty to grumbling. When that sort of professional jealousy breaks out, you can choose between two basic attitudes: discontentment and complaining, or contentment and gratitude. You can respond by saying, "I've spent as much money getting my doctorate as they have. I teach just as many courses. And none of them have been here twice as long as I have. So why can't the administration be as generous with me as with them?" Or you can say, "Thank God we're going to have qualified teachers to teach our students in every department. That's what this institution is all about." You must choose which way you *will* react.

Life is filled with this type thing. You probably have a friend who makes more money than you do. He lives in a larger house and drives a finer car than you (even though you're obviously smarter and more talented than he is). How you handle the difference depends on your attitude. If you're always comparing yourself and your situation to others, you'll always be discontent. You'll spend all your time at a personal pity party that will destroy your happiness and contentment. But you can choose to rejoice in the good fortune of others, and you will spend your life rejoicing and happy "whatever the circumstances."

My Fair Share

Jesus tells a story about some folks who always insisted on getting their "fair share." He reveals that their rotten attitudes arose from faulty reasoning. The owner of a vineyard hired a group of workers for a day and agreed to pay them a stipulated wage. They were to work 12 hours, from 6 a.m. to 6 p.m., for that wage.

At 9 a.m. the owner found some more workers and put them to work with the promise that he would pay them what was right. At noon and again at 3 a.m. he found more idle men and hired them to start to work immediately with the same arrangement. Finally, at 5 p.m. he found yet other workers, and he asked them to work for just the last hour of the day.

Why would the owner of the vineyard hire a group of men to work for only an hour? There might be a lot of different reasons. Perhaps, he had compassion on the workers and hired them for their benefit, not his. Or, he may have seen that the only way he could meet his daily harvest quota was to add more hands at the last minute. The reason is not really important.

When the wages were given out at the end of the day, every man received the same pay. That's when the trouble broke loose. There were those who just murmured. Some complained long and loud. And some probably filed a grievance with their local vineyard workers' union representative. And who do you think grumbled the most? Right. It was the workers who had been on the job the longest. They not only thought they should have more money, but they also began complaining about the working conditions, like excessive heat.

The owner was able to answer their charges, though, with an irrefutable argument that made their grievances look silly. He turned to one of the workers and said, "My friend, I'm not being unfair to you. Didn't you agree to work for this amount? Take your pay and go. I want to give the man who was hired last the same as I gave you. Don't I have the right to do what I want with my own money? Or are you envious because I am generous" (Matthew 20:1-16)?

The owner of the vineyard in this parable represents God. The kindness he exhibited to the workers hired at the end of the day was the same kindness that had caused him to hire the workers early in the day. It wasn't the owner who had the problem; it was the workers. It was their attitude toward his kindness that was faulty, and it led them into discontentment. They were perfectly content with their working conditions and their pay until they compared themselves with others. The problems arose from their false assumption that seniority on the job would be the basis for salaries, rather than the owner's generosity. It is interesting (and revealing) that those workers who had an ironclad financial agreement were the ones to grumble about their pay, while those who were hired on a promise of right treatment were content.

Jesus makes it clear in this story that God does not give his gifts to us based on how hard or how long we work for him. From beginning to end he treats each of us with a generosity and kindness far greater than we deserve. If he dealt with us on the basis of what we deserve, we would find ourselves in dire circumstances indeed. But God gives to each of us what it pleases him to give us. If he gave us special privileges, he knows we would always be jealous of each other. Knowing that he treats each of us kindly and better than we deserve to be treated, we are left with but one logical attitude: Apart from God we would have nothing.

Happiness comes from being content with what we *have*, not what we don't have or wish we had. When it gets right down to it, we ought to be mighty grateful that most all of us have what few of the kings themselves had a hundred years ago — a warm house, hot water, a warm wife and bifocals.

Change Your Way of Thinking

Now that you *believe* you can change, and you've decided you *will* change, you'll most likely have to change the *way you think*. Fundamentally, our challenge is to learn how Christ thought and then make his thoughts our own. The Bible says it this way: ". . . take captive every thought to make it obedient to Christ" (2 Corinthians 10:5).

"You can change motivation and improve performance by changing the way you . . . think," says David McClelland after a 25-year research study conducted at Harvard University.

The Come Down Attitude

The ultimate maturity is to think like Christ. But what is the mind of Christ? How does he think? Paul reveals exactly how the Godhead thinks in Philippians 2. The church at Philippi had a problem between two co-workers of Paul. Seeking resolution and peace, he calls on them to "have the mind of Christ." One translation says "the attitude of Christ."

The first thing that comes to Paul's mind is the incarnation — how God came down from Godhood to manhood. We can call this the "come down" attitude. God came down from heaven to earth. Even as man he didn't place himself in a king's bassinet but in a stable's feeding trough. The humility to come down as a carpenter's helper with no formal education or prestige is the model.

He invites us to join him washing feet and in service to others from the "one down" position. We Americans don't like the "one down' position. We fight for our rights and the "one up" position — a position of strength and power. But power, real power, comes from within, not without. So our thinking must change! Strength, power, confidence and assurance from within — enough to be weak and humble without — this is the mind of Christ. And this is just the opposite, I fear, of our American culture. Notice what Paul said:

> Do nothing out of selfish ambition or vain conceit, but in humility consider others better than yourselves. Each of you should look not only to your own interests, but also to the interests of others. Your attitude should be the same as that of Christ Jesus: Who, being in very nature God, did not consider equality with God something to be grasped, but made himself nothing, taking the very nature of a servant, being made in human likeness. And being found in appearance as a man, he humbled himself and became obedient to death — even death on a cross! Therefore God exalted him to the highest place and gave him the name that is above every name, that at the name of Jesus every knee should bow, in heaven and on earth and under the earth, and every tongue confess that Jesus Christ is Lord, to the glory of God the Father (Philippians 2:3-11).

Reframing — A Way to Change

One way to change your thinking is to reframe the way you perceive the circumstances that surround you until you can think of them in their most positive and favorable light. An artist can take an ordinary-looking picture and, by putting a decorative color-coordinated frame around it, completely transform the picture. You look at the reframed picture and think, "My, I didn't really see that picture's beauty until it was framed." That's the gift of an artist. He has learned to display his handiwork in its most attractive form. Life can be reframed, too!

Marion Kaywood moved to West Texas to teach voice in a university. In a welcome-to-Texas bit of hospitality, we had a little breakfast in her honor in the backyard of a fellow professor. Now, Marion's from the gorgeous state of Kentucky where the beautiful green trees tower into the sky and the blue grass grows in such lush abundance. And we're sitting in West Texas where the dust blows because there are only a few dinky sage brush and scrubby Mesquites to hold it down. Quite a contrast.

So I asked Marion that morning, half dreading the response, "How do you like West Texas?"

She smiled from ear to ear and replied in her lovely, lilting voice that distinguished her from the rest of us, "Oh, I love it! I just love it! All those tall trees in Kentucky would get in the way of these beautiful West Texas sunsets."

Did she mean that she didn't appreciate the Kentucky trees? No. She simply meant that she had also found something beautiful about West Texas. She had looked past the blowing dirt, the scraggly grass, the scrubby trees and tumbling weeds and focused on one of the few redeeming features of West Texas — the glorious sunsets. She had simply reframed the picture to bring out its best qualities.

That's the way to change your attitude. Reframe the things around you until you can see them in their best light.

Biblical Reframing

The book of James urges us to reframe our thinking this way: "Consider it pure joy, my brothers, whenever you face trials of many kinds." That seems illogical. Why should we be happy about hard times? "Because you know that the testing of your faith develops perseverance. Perseverance must finish its work so that you may be mature and complete, not lacking anything" (James 1:2-4).

I like the way J. B. Phillips translated it: "When all kinds of trials and temptations crowd into your lives, my brothers, don't resent them as intruders, but welcome them as friends."

And 2 Corinthians 4:7-9 emphasizes it again: "But we have this treasure in jars of clay to show that this all-surpassing power is from God and not from us. We are hard pressed on every side, but not crushed; perplexed, but not in despair; persecuted, but not abandoned; struck down, but not destroyed."

But what if something horrible, a real catastrophe, happens to you. Can you reframe catastrophe? A friend of mine was mugged and shot full in the face by a man on a downtown metropolitan street. The bullet shattered her lower jaw. She saved her own life by using the shattered jaw as a compress to partially check the profuse bleeding. As a result of the tragedy, she resigned from a high-paying executive position in an oil company, out of consideration for the company, not because she was asked to.

I saw her a while back, and the conversation fell into a discussion of this past incident. I said, "You must really resent that guy."

Surprisingly, she answered, "No, I had to work through those feelings." Then she grinned, pointed to her chin and said, "Say, have you seen my new dimple?"

If a catastrophe like that happened to you, could you handle it as well? Many would allow such an incident to rob them of happiness and contentment for the rest of their lives. But my friend shows that it doesn't have to be that way. You can reframe your thinking and find the dimple in the disaster.

Strength in Weakness

I am reminded of the apostle Paul who learned to be content in any situation and who lived day by day with an agonizing pain that he called a "thorn in the flesh." Three times this servant, who often brought healing to others, asked the Lord to remove the painful thorn from his body. But there was only silence. The last time I think I hear Paul saying, "Lord, you don't understand. I'm not asking you to remove this from me for selfish reasons. If I could get rid of this pain (or, perhaps, disfigurement), I would have more strength and reputation to tell others about your will. I could do a much better job of glorifying your name."

And the Lord answered Paul, in essence: "Paul, you're asking me to give you strength by removing the thorn in your flesh. But what you don't understand about my strength is that it comes from weakness" (2 Corinthians 12:7-10).

"You mean, Lord, that your strength is given to me through this thorn?" asks Paul. Yes, through the thorn (or the dimple in your chin). It may come through being physically disabled like Robert, or who knows what else. To reframe the weakness as a strength is having the mind of Christ.

Have you ever said to the Lord, or the people around you, "I can't because I'm too old"? "I can't because I'm in poor health." "I can't because I'm grieving over the loss of a loved one." "I can't because of . . . this tragedy or that problem." But you *can*, because God strengthens those who trust him explicitly.

"Well, if that's the way it is, Lord," Paul seemed to say, "then send me more thorns so your grace may abound toward me." That's a tough prayer to pray. But that's where contentment is found. It's found in an attitude that says, "Not as I will, but as you will" (Matthew 26:39). Or, "I can do everything through him who gives me strength" (Philippians 4:13).

Change Your Actions

To change your attitude you must *believe* that you can change. You must *will* to change. You must change your perceptions and the *way* you think. Then comes the toughest challenge of all: You must change your *actions*.

Having the mind of Christ is like a great musical masterpiece that's been conceived in the mind of its composer and recorded on paper as a musical score. To become beautiful music it doesn't require additional instructions or explanations. It requires rendition. It must be played or sung! It requires action.

Your responsibility as a person of faith is to let Christ within you express the actions of his mind through you. This should be as natural and automatic as breathing.

An accomplished clarinetist doesn't look at a quarter note on the first space of the treble clef and reason out: "The note on the first space of the treble clef is called 'f,' and in order to play it I must cover the 'f' hole on the bottom of my clarinet with the thumb of my left hand, blow air between the mouthpiece and reed of my instrument and hold it for one full count." A beginning clarinet student might do that, but it makes noise, not music. Not until he learns to read music several measures in advance and learns to adjust his fingers and control the length and flow of air being pushed through his clarinet without conscious thought or effort can he become a real musician. And like any other great art, that skill requires practice.

Fritz Kreisler, the great violinist, was once approached after a concert by a lady who said, "I'd give my life to play like you do."

Mr. Kreisler simply replied, "That's exactly what I did, lady."

If you are serious about having the mind of Christ, there is no substitute for practicing the *actions* of his life. You must give your very life to becoming a great Christian. You must *act* like one . . . spontaneously . . . automatically. It must be second nature to you, like breathing.

The Say-Yes Face

President Thomas Jefferson was riding horseback with some companions, and they came to a swollen stream. A foot traveler was there by the stream, waiting to ask someone on horseback to give him a ride across the rushing water. The President responded to the man's request. He pulled the man up on his horse and later set him down on the opposite bank.

"Tell me," asked one of the men, "why did you ask the President to help you across?"

The man answered, "I didn't know he was the President. All I know is that on some faces is written the answer 'no,' and on some is written the answer 'yes.' He had a *yes* face."

What you put in your heart will reflect in your attitudes and actions. If you have the mind of Christ, the *yes* attitude of Christ will show on your face and in your actions. Be more thoughtful than necessary, kinder than necessary, more compassionate and sympathetic than necessary. Keep practicing it and doing it, and people will begin to see that attitude written on your face.

"When he saw the multitudes, he was moved with compassion on them, because they were as sheep having no shepherd" (Matthew 9:36). His compassion for people could be seen in his eyes and read on his face. You can change your face by changing your attitudes and actions.

USE IT OR LOSE IT

If you put your arm in a sling and keep it inactive, soon it becomes limp and useless. The fish in Mammoth Cave are blind because they do not use their eyes. Stop acting in faith, and faith dies. Stop hoping, and hope dies. Use it or lose it—that's the message.

When I speak with appreciation of my wife and children, my attitude of appreciation toward them increases. When I go out of my way to do something that puts the interest of someone else above my own, my attitude of goodwill toward that person grows. When I express my love for God through my actions, the attitude of love for God blooms.

It's sort of like the burnt thank offerings God required of his people in Old Testament times. He didn't need the food they brought or the smoke from the offering. But he knew that the people needed to express their thanks to him through *actions*, and this was a tangible way to do it.

So, put on your coveralls, roll up your shirt sleeves, and let's get the attitudes of Christ off the pages of a book and into operation in your life. Let the beautiful music of your heart praise God through your actions.

CHANGE YOUR DISPOSITION

It's been one of those Murphy-was-an-optimist kind of days. Your 2-year-old son flushed a sock down the toilet, and your bathtub is filling up from the backflow of the clogged drain. You're in the midst of yelling at your repentent and crying child when the phone rings. It's a Boris Karloff voice wanting to sell you a pre-need funeral plan for Restlawn Cemetery. Resenting the interruption to your private emotional explosion, you curtly inform the caller that you don't buy anything over the telephone and slam down the receiver.

The slam of the receiver snaps you back to reality, and you realize how rude and unfeeling you acted toward the caller. Quickly you ask God to forgive your unseemly behavior. And you think, "May God bless you, friend. May God rest your soul."

The phone rings again. You pick it up and with a honey-calmed voice you say, "Hellooooo!" Your boss says, "Hey, am I interrupting anything?" And you sweetly respond, "Oh, nooo! I'm so *glad* you called." And you're as happy as a pig in the sunshine.

What happened? You changed your attitude and, by changing your attitude, your disposition. Just like that! Faster than a speeding bullet! You see, you can take control of your thoughts and attitudes and change them, all in an instant. God has given you the power to make things right, even when everything is going all wrong.

When Do You Get Happy?

There's this boy in junior high school. He doesn't seem to have a care in the world. A fellow says, "You're a happy guy, aren't you?" He says, "No, sir. If only I had a girlfriend, I'd have it made."

Now he's in high school and going steady with a girl. The fellow says, "You're a happy guy now." He says, "No, it doesn't do much good to have a girlfriend if you don't have wheels. If only I had a car, I'd be happy."

Now the boy has a car, a girlfriend—the whole bit. And the fellow says, "Well, you've got it made now." And the boy replies, "I'm not sure about that. If only I could go to college, get my degree and get married, then I'd be happy for sure."

The fellow sees him a few years later. The boy's graduated from college and married. So he says, "Surely, you've got it made now." He replies, "No, but if I only had a good job and could make a down payment on a house, I'd be the happiest guy you ever saw."

The fellow sees him later in front of his new house and says, "At last, you're happy, right?" "No, sir. Have you ever tried to raise teenagers? If I could just get my kids through college, I'd have it made." And later he complains, "I don't have adequate retirement. If I could just buy me a little place up in Arkansas to retire and raise a few chickens, I'd have it made."

Would you believe it? The fellow is driving down a little gravel road up in the Ozark Mountains in Arkansas years later and sees that same guy. He's sitting in his rocking chair on the porch of a neat little white house. Out back are some chicken houses. He gets out, runs up to the guy on the porch and says with a big smile, "Wow! Here it is. It's everything you've ever wanted, worked for, struggled for and paid for.

You've really got it made now!" The old man says, "But I've got rheumatism, my wife's got lumbago, and the hens aren't laying. But one of these days, in the sweet by and by, I'm going to be a truly happy man."

This old fool is never going to be happy! Even if he makes it to heaven, his halo will probably be too tight, and all that singing will get on his nerves. His grumbling and griping would exhaust the patience of Job and the wisdom of Solomon.

"All the days of the oppressed are wretched," when you live under the illusion that happiness comes only when circumstances get better, "but the cheerful heart has a continual feast" (Proverbs 15:15). A happy heart makes a happy life. And your attitudes determine the happiness of your heart.

EYES OF THE LORD

"For the eyes of the Lord range throughout the earth to strengthen those whose hearts are fully committed to him" (2 Chronicles 16:9). Folks, he's looking for someone whose heart is centered on him so he can empower them to greatness. He's looking for the person who has the mind of Christ. He's looking for the person who has changed his attitudes and his actions to match the attitudes and actions of Christ. He's looking to see if you have had the courage to grab your *wanter* by your *willer* and take control of your attitude.

What are we saying? We're saying that you're just one attitude away from having a fantastic life. We're saying that you can make things right when they go wrong by changing your attitude. God has given you the power to reach out, grasp that fantastic life and make things right. So, go for it!

It is easier to act yourself into a better way of feeling than to feel yourself into a better way of acting.
— O. H. Mowrer

People curse us, but we bless them. They persecute us, and we endure it. They say evil things against us, but we say only kind things to them.
— 1 Corinthians 4:9-13

CHAPTER THREE

Act Better Than You Feel

Wouldn't it be wonderful if you always *felt* like doing what you *ought* to do?

"Honey, the yard needs mowing, and you need to clean up after the dog."

"Oh, good," you say. "That's exactly what I want to do."

"Sweetheart, the clothes need to be ironed, and the bathroom needs cleaning."

And you say, "Great! How did you know that's what I've been waiting to do?"

If life worked like that, you wouldn't have nearly so many problems. But life has its uncanny way of hurling you into situations where you must act better than you feel. Following your feelings often leaves important things undone. And it's so easy for feelings to misfire, lash out and cause devastating results. But there's good news: you can make things right when they've gone wrong by acting better than you feel.

It reminds me of the manager of a fast food store who had urged the lad working at the counter to "act friendly." But the boy continued treating the customers with little or no courtesy.

So, the manager stated his request a bit stronger: "Son, you really *must* be more friendly to the customers." And this time he noticed a very slight improvement in the lad's manners, but it wasn't enough yet.

Finally, the manager demanded: "You've got to act friendly!"

Promptly, almost angrily, the young man shot back: "I am friendly! They just can't see it."

But the manager was right; the boy's actions spoke much louder than his words. The boy's *act* was not as convincing as it needed to be.

JUST DO IT!

Do you like slick okra? You know, the slimy boiled kind. Well, me neither when I was growing up, but there is a way you can learn to eat that slick green stuff and like it. You have to say to yourself, "Eating boiled okra is beneficial to my health, and I'm going to keep on eating it and acting as if I like it until I do like it, even if it kills me!"

The attitude to *want to* like it *plus the action* to seal the commitment will work six times out of ten (nine times out of ten, if you don't give up too soon). You have to just *do* it. You have to act better than you feel about it.

If I ate and drank only what I *felt* like eating and drinking, my diet would most likely be limited to Snicker bars, Dr. Peppers and those big Fritos. So, in the interest of nutrition, I have learned to eat *and like* many other beverages and foods. It has broadened my narrow-minded taste buds.

My wife Gladys and I went to Brazil to work with some missionaries and their families. One lovely couple took us to a restaurant that was famous for the Brazilian national dish called *Feijoada*. It reminded us of what we southerners call hamhock and beans. Of course, the beans didn't look exactly like the kind of beans we eat, and the meat didn't look exactly like ham. But Gladys took some beans from the bowl anyway and was about to take a piece of meat when one of the missionaries said, "Gladys, you'd better put your glasses on." Well, she slipped on her glasses and found she was about to do battle with a pig's snout, its two upturned nostrils pointing right at her. Bless her heart, I was so proud. She just thought "ham" and ate it — not because she *felt* like eating it, but because she thought she *ought* to eat it and act as if she was enjoying what the Brazilians eat. Sure enough, *Feijoada* grew on us; and later we treated our taste buds to other culinary delights.

Guess what Gladys and I ate in China. We ate many things, but would you believe they included squid, octopus, eel, dog and baby sparrows that you pop into your mouth whole and just eat them bones, crunch and all — and with chopsticks? That last little item on the menu may get to you. It did us. In fact, I must be honest, the one item we *didn't* eat was the sparrow. We didn't score a perfect 10, but we got close. Be assured that your actions toward people will eventually change your attitudes toward them. I believe that's why we fell in love with the people of China.

FAKE IT 'TIL YOU MAKE IT

You may be thinking: "Faulkner, acting better than you feel is hypocrisy." But you are a hypocrite only when you deceive others into thinking you are what you *never intend* to become, like an insurance salesman who goes to church to make sales rather than to become a better Christian. In contrast, acting out a part on the stage of life because you honestly desire to adopt the noble qualities of that character springs from genuine motives, not hypocrisy.

Members of Alcoholics Anonymous use a motto to encourage each other to succeed: "Fake it 'til you make it." You can be sure these people are not using the term "fake" in a phony or hypocritical sense. Their intent is to make it. Their intent is to fake the feeling that they don't want a drink, one day at a time. "Acting as if" they are recovered alcoholics, they cast themselves in the direction of sobriety, until they really make it.

Hypothesis, Not Hypocrisy

The hypothesis is, "If you will keep acting as if you like to do what you do not want to do, the time will come when you will like and want to do it."

O. H. Mowrer said: "It is easier to act yourself into a better way of feeling than to feel yourself into a better way of acting." That's so good.

I also like the way William James put it: "You don't sing because you are happy, you are happy because you sing."

It's like a mother awakened in the middle of the night by her crying baby. What mother would say to her baby: "Honey, I'm sorry I can't get up and change your diaper right now because I don't want to be a hypocrite—I just don't feel like changing your diaper." No, a loving mom fakes it—feel like it or not! She gets up, changes the diaper, feeds and burps "little darling" who smiles, coos and then drops off to sleep. And how does mom feel now? Chances are nine-to-one that she feels great when she crawls back under the covers. You always feel better (on the inside) when you have acted responsibly. Most of the good in this world is done by those who don't feel like it.

Frank B. Minirth and Paul D. Meier, psychiatrists who have written extensively about depression, said in their book *Happiness Is a Choice*: "Just be sure that behavior will ultimately change your feelings." If you are depressed, get your mind off yourself (counselors frequently call this *navel gazing*), and do things to bless other people. The chances are that in a short time happiness will return to you.

Dr. George Crane said it well: "If you go through the motion, you'll feel the emotion." Never ask Aunt Gertie, "How ya' been *feelin'*?" Rather, ask her, "Whatcha been *doin'*?" Home in on her actions (external-others) instead of her feelings (internal-self).

Waitin' For The Urge?

The odds are overwhelming that you will never do what you ought to do if you wait for the urge to strike.

A lumberjack and his axe were leaning against a tree one day, and some folks passing by asked him: "Hey, when are you going to chop wood? We want to see a real axeman lay down a tree."

His answer? "When I work up a sweat."

Well, there's no valve that will turn on sweat. He'll have to start chopping first. Neither is there a valve to turn on a feeling. It's impossible to *will* a feeling. You can never expect to feel great by just saying: "I'm going to *will* myself to feel great." But you *can* will an *action* that will make you feel great.

Let me level with you. If I had waited for the urge this morning, I would not have gotten out of bed at 6 a.m. to write these lines. By nature and temperament, I'm a night person. Mornings are not my thing. I throw one leg out of bed, and if it survives, I throw out the other leg. Then an arm. But when I finally get all my parts assembled in a standing position and the blood circulating, I feel downright cocky and proud. I don't feel like getting up early, but I feel good once I've done it.

Ernest Newman, an English music critic, said: "The great composer does not set to work because he is inspired, but *becomes* inspired because he is working. Beethoven, Bach, Mozart settled down day after day to the job at hand with as much regularity as an accountant settles down each day to his figures. They didn't waste time waiting for inspiration."

LISTEN TO YOUR THINKER

The brains drag the guts. Gladys isn't too crazy about that expression, but maybe you'll remember it. Listen to your "thinker," and do what it tells you to do, and the right attitudes and feelings will follow along. God didn't give you a "feeler" to tell you what to do! He designed your brain for that function. Your feelings rejoice when your brain has done what it ought to do because your "feeler" understands that your "thinker" knows best.

Listening to your feelings will blow your diet, bring failure to your job, distract you from your goals and destroy your marriage. Young couples come to me day after day with marriages in trouble because they entered into marriage based on their "feelers" instead of their "thinkers." They discover through sad experience that good feelings toward one another before marriage cannot long sustain the relationship because romantic *impulses* are not adequate substitutes for positive *actions* of love. In evaluating a future mate, listen to your "thinker" instead of your "feeler."

ACT AS IF - THE CHANGE AGENT

By changing your actions, you can actually change your attitudes and the way you think. One psychologist observed: "Behavior causes attitudes. There is now sufficient evidence to suggest that . . . one of the most effective ways to change hearts and minds of men is to change their behavior."

One technique I use with fighting couples is to have them tell me all the good they can think of about each other, not the bad. Then I suggest, "I want you to work at acting like a happy couple. Whether you feel like it or not, just act that way." This "act as if" principle softens the harshness of the relationship. The logic is that "acting as if" for a few weeks gives the therapist the needed atmosphere for him to set in motion other techniques that will accomplish their mutual goal. Most *dysfunctional* (that's a two-dollar word that means something isn't working right) couples are so negative that growth is stunted.

"Acting as if" allows you to transcend and transform your own nature — to do what's *un*natural until it becomes natural.

And It Really Works

Here is an excerpt from a letter I received: "You were so right that you *can* act yourself into a better way of thinking, but I didn't really believe it. So I picked an area where there was still some hope."

(The area she chose was the sexual area — an area that I would most likely have discouraged at the time — nevertheless, listen to what follows.)

> It is so exciting to sit here and type this and think about the change that has come over our relationship since I began to look forward to the time I spend with my husband . . . It is so amazing the way it works . . .
>
> And it's funny because all the things that I held on to as urgent, important, necessary . . . things that needed to be dealt with every evening before we went to bed (money, children, family, work), *are taking care of themselves.* I'm a more pleasant person, and my husband feels loved, really loved.
>
> And it's so amazing how it affects every other area of our lives. We both seem to accomplish more. We get along with everyone around us better (children, friends, extended family).

THE SNOWBALL THEORY

Just let one person do the right thing, whether they feel like it or not, and it inevitably sets in motion an avalanche of other good things. It snowballs!

Bret Hart tells a story about the change that occurred in a mining camp in California. It started with a rather small but significant action . . . and spread!

A woman with a questionable reputation, the only woman in the whole camp, died. She left behind a small baby, and the men of the camp had to take care of it. The baby was lying in a box. The men felt that a box was not fit for a baby's crib. So they sent one of their members 80 miles on a mule to Sacramento to get a rosewood cradle. When the cradle came, the rags in which the baby was sleeping seemed out of place. So the man was sent back to Sacramento to purchase some lacy, frilly clothes. When the baby was dressed in the lovely clothes and placed in the rosewood cradle, the men observed for the first time that the floor was dirty. So they scrubbed it. Then they noticed that the walls and ceiling were unsightly. So they proceeded to whitewash them. Afterward, they repaired the windows and draped them. And because the baby needed sleep and rest, they remained quiet and stopped some of their rough language and rowdy ways.

When the weather permitted, they took the cradle up to the mines. But they discovered that the mining area had to be cleaned and flowers planted to make the surroundings lovely and attractive for the baby. Finally, the men began to improve their own personal appearance. Thus, the coming of a baby, and a sense of responsibility and obligation to it, snowballed to transform Roaring Mine Camp into a new and attractive place.

How Our Fortnight Became a Tradition

Let me tell you more about this "snowball" theory. The more you "act as if," the easier it gets. The further you push a snowball, the bigger it gets; and the further you push yourself to do what you don't want to do, the more you actually enjoy it. It gets on a roll.

One Friday evening late, Gladys said: "Paul, let's jump up real early in the morning and go to the Neiman Marcus Fortnight in Dallas!"

Each year the Dallas store features a foreign country on all six floors: entertainment, housewares, stationery, clothing, toys and food. It had been a delightful experience when we were in Dallas for a seminar. But, this time we were at home — three and a half hours away. It was the last thing on my mind. I was thinking, "Stay home, relax, play tennis, do a little yard work." But I acted better than I felt and said: "Sure, honey, let's give it a go." (I surprised myself!)

We arrived at the store early the next morning and picked up a program: "French Fortnight at Neiman's." After I marked all the things "we" wanted to see, we began touring. When we were apart for a few minutes, I got in a long line. Now, I *know* I was acting beyond myself because I hate lines. But she loves French pastry. When she saw me in the pastry shop line, the biggest smile I ever saw lit up her face.The smile was *more* than worth the long line. (Acting as if is getting easier now — snowballing right along.)

I even went to see the weird French dresses with her. Then she went with me to see the French-made autos (acting better than *she* felt, I think). You see, you don't go around telling the other person you are "acting as if," 'cause then you don't get a good feelin' inside.

After lunch she said she would like another hour and a half to see some things she had missed. I agreed to meet her at the car at 3 p.m. But she didn't show up at 3:00 . . . or 3:15 . . . or 3:30 . . . or 3:45. When she came up 50 minutes late, kinda cute like, half running and apologizing all over the place, I was at my *prime* (because I hate waiting for late people)! I said, "No sweat." (I was really outdoing myself! I have never acted so content under similar circumstances.) But it was the truth. I had finished grading a set of papers and was listening to a Saturday football game. It's getting easier and easier to enjoy myself.

But then Gladys said: "Paul, this is such a beautiful day; let's find some place to enjoy nature."

Nature! Enjoy nature! But, before my ol' self could pout, I found myself saying, "Well, how about the Botanical Gardens in Fort Worth!" (The Gardens are on the way back home — a double purpose, but still legit.)

The gardens were simply beautiful! Two wedding parties were taking pictures, and another wedding was in progress among the roses. I actually enjoyed it immensely! "Now we can go home," I thought. I'm like an old rent horse—when I have done my turn, I head for the barn.

But a sweet voice overrode my thoughts: "Now where shall we eat?" (She'd been hitting home runs all day. Why stop now?)

My first thought was to eat at McDonald's on the way back home. "Well, let's just drive around and see," I said. (Amazed at myself!) I drove around three different places—one was expensive, the others moderate. You guessed it. We ate at the more expensive Swiss Chalet. (Well, after all, we had eaten at Walgreens for lunch, hadn't we?) It was a super decision. The Chalet was down by the river, and the meal was served with impeccable grace.

"Paul, you know what I would like to do?" (By now the snowball is really big, and I'm really loving it, but how can this be? It's late, and we're 150 miles from home.) "I would just like to sit here with coffee and dessert, look at the river and talk as long as we want to talk." So we did; and when we got in the car, there was our kind of music on the radio; and when we arrived home (Who cared what time it was?), we watched a delightful T. V. movie. It had been one of those perfect days.

But did it all just happen? Was it all luck? We think it was because we *chose* to act better than we felt. Then the good feelings caught up with us and began to snowball. I began the day thinking, "I don't want to," but that night in bed I said to Gladys: "Let's go to Neiman's Fortnight every year. We'll make it a tradition!" We have other traditions that were made the same way. Acting better than you feel—don't knock it 'til you've tried it!

COGNITIVE DISSONANCE—WHAT'S THAT?

"When two *cognitions* (beliefs) are *dissonant* (in opposition to each other), the one which is reinforced by behavioral consistency will become stronger . . . I will tend to believe more deeply those assumptions which are consistent with the way I behave," suggests Leon Festinger, noted researcher.

You're suffering from *cognitive dissonance* when you are pulled between two conflicting beliefs or desires. The little child part of you may be sitting on your shoulder whispering in your ear: "Go ahead and eat the ice cream." But the adult part of you is saying, "No, it will make you fat."

We see this cognitive dissonance in the life of the apostle Paul in Romans 7:15 when he wrote: "What I want to do I do not do, but what I hate I do." Have you ever felt like that? The things that you don't want to do, you do. The things you want to do, you don't do. This causes frustration, anxiety and confusion.

How do you get rid of cognitive dissonance? Well, you can either change belief number one ("I want the car") until it squares up with belief number two ("I can't afford it"), or you can change belief number two until it squares up with belief number one. You mean you can change either one of them in either direction? Yes! How? Festinger says it depends on which belief you most consistently *act* upon. Your repeated, determined actions actually can change your beliefs.

ACTIONS SEAL COMMITMENT

During the winter of 1835-36, the people of Texas decided to sever their relations with the government of Mexico. To prevent this, the Mexican government, late in February 1836, sent General Antonio Lopez de Santa Anna with over 2,000 troops to the Texas settlement of San Antonio. The city had a force of about 188 men under Lieutenant William Barret Travis. The company included heroes like James Bowie and David Crockett. The arrival of the Mexicans took the Texans by surprise. They retreated to the Alamo to make their stand. Travis sent out a messenger with a letter containing a plea for help and declaring, "I shall never surrender or retreat."

The siege of the Alamo began on February 23, 1836. By March 5, the garrison could not return Mexican fire because ammunition had run low. This convinced Santa Anna that the fort could be assaulted. During the night, the Mexican general ordered his men to place ladders on the walls of the fort so they might be scaled the following morning.

In the crisis of that hour, Travis assembled his company and said, in essence: "Men, I am not asking for your loyalty. I am asking for your life. We can't win the battle, but we can delay the Mexican army and save the State."

He then unsheathed his sabre and used its point to draw a line on the floor of the Alamo. He said, "All who are willing to stay and fight, step across the line."

Everyone stepped across but two men. James Bowie couldn't step across. He was so ill and weak that he could not arise from his cot. But he said to his comrades: "Men, pick me up and set me over the line." They did.

When the brave men ran out of ammunition, they used their muskets as clubs in losing the battle which cost them their lives. *Their actions sealed their commitment.*

THERE IS A PRICE FOR FEELING BETTER

Jesus sealed his commitment to us and paid the price on the cross. Where do we get the idea that God put us on earth to indulge our feelings? He promises us a cross, not cushions, and scars, not medals. He makes it clear that if we are not willing to nail ourselves to the cross again and again and act better than we feel—willing to pay the *price* for the *privilege* of following him — he would rather that we not follow him at all. He has never admired the lukewarm attitude (see Revelation 3:16).

Jesus said, "Love your enemies, and pray for those who persecute you" (Matthew 5:44). Do you *feel* like loving your enemy? Do you feel like doing good things for that guy who takes advantage of you and does you wrong? No, but it enables you to do the will of God, by blessing your enemies, and at the same time you achieve a personal victory.

The apostles followed the model of Christ. Listen to Paul's message: "People curse us, but we bless them." (They are acting better than they feel, aren't they?) "They persecute us, and we endure it." (That's tough and doesn't feel good either.) "They say evil things against us, but we say only kind things to them" (1 Corinthians 4:9-13).

THE STORY OF TWO JEWS

When the Romans conquered a nation, it was their custom to place a yoke in the center of each city symbolizing submission to Roman rule. They would then install mile markers radiating out from the yoke along the nation's roads. These mile markers indicated the distance (one mile) a Roman soldier could require a conquered citizen to carry his pack.

Picture a Jew chopping weeds in his field. He calls himself a Christian, but his negative attitude denies it. He's complaining to God because it hasn't rained, and he's cursing the weeds that have taken over his crop when a Roman soldier spies him and shouts: "You, come over here and carry my load!"

This forced intrusion really sets him off. He throws down his hoe, trudges to the road and snatches up the load — breaking the strap. He blames the strap, claiming it was weak. The Roman soldier cuffs him and forces him to carry the bag without a strap, which is most difficult. After hearing him fret, fume and denounce the Roman government for the entire mile, the Roman soldier is glad to send him back.

Our "Christian" man is in a depression now and even further behind in his work. He returns to the field to find his hoe is broken (from his having thrown it down in disgust). He storms home.

His wife meets him: "Hi, honey, home early?"

"Don't honey me, just get out of my sight!"

The children come around the house: "Daddy's home! Daddy's home!"

"I thought I told you to feed the chickens!" he shouts. This family is headed for a wonderful evening, huh?

Not far down the road, the Roman spots another Jew. Not wishing to encounter another belligerent Jew, but reluctant to tote his bag with a broken strap, he shouts to the man in the field: "Come carry this bag!"

To his surprise, the Jew quickly puts down his hoe and almost runs to the road to help the soldier. The first thing the Jew notices is the broken strap. He volunteers that he has an awl and leather and can fix it promptly, if the soldier will just wait in the shade of that tree.

They haven't walked a hundred yards before the soldier knows this Jew is like none he has ever met before. He is animated and engaging. Before he knows it, the soldier is talking about his family as if he were an old friend.

It seems only a few minutes when the soldier says: "Oh, I'm sorry. You have carried my pack a mile and a half."

"I know," said the Jew, "but it seemed only a half mile. Ever since I met the Carpenter, my whole outlook on life has changed; everything and everybody seem different, for some reason."

The soldier had already noticed. "This Carpenter," the soldier said, "who is he? Where is he from?"

They had already gone two miles by now, and the Jew explained that he really must get back. But he noted: "You are headed straight into Capernaum where the Carpenter is teaching. Please join the crowd; I'll bet he will make a difference in your life, too."

He returned home, almost skipping as he went. He picked up his hoe, and it seemed so light he just flew through the rest of the weeds.

"Hi, honey, you're home early."

"Yes," he replied, "and where are my precious children?"

She said: "Ah, I know what's up . . . you come in smiling, with that gleam in your eye; you have been another second mile, haven't you?"

THE REAL HEROES

This "act as if" principle boils down to faith. Act better than you feel, and act as if every tomorrow will be better than today, even when common sense tells you otherwise, and they will be.

Heroes of faith did this with fantastic results:

> And what more shall I say? I do not have time to tell about Gideon, Barak, Samson, Jephthah, David, Samuel and the prophets, who through faith conquered kingdoms, administered justice, and gained what was promised; who shut the mouths of lions, quenched the fury of the flames, and escaped the edge of the sword; whose weakness was turned to strength; and who became powerful in battle and routed foreign armies" (Hebrews 11:32-34).

"Faith is being sure of what we hope for and certain of what we do not see" (Hebrews 11:1). That's the "act as if" principle in a nutshell.

If what you came to do, you did, then you can say, "It's finished." You must learn to say, "I came to do my father's will." And then do it!

The pull to get off course is not just between good and bad; sometimes it's between good and good.

CHAPTER FOUR

Use Your Compass When You're Off Course

Novelist George Moore tells how the government put the peasants to work building roads during the great depression in Ireland. Delighted to have jobs again, they worked energetically, singing songs with zest, until one day they realized what was happening — the road they were building didn't go anywhere. It just rambled out into the countryside and stopped in the middle of nowhere. The road was useless. The government had put them to work just to give them something to do. The songs stopped, and the workers became listless. Moore observed, "The roads to nowhere are difficult to make. For a man to work and sing, there must be an end in view."

What is your aim in life? What is your one great dream that gives your life direction, significance and a sense of purpose? Have you checked in with God to see if your master ambition is as big as the one he has chosen for you? Have you hitched your wagon to the right star?

Be careful about the target you choose. If you aim at nothing, you'll hit the bull's-eye every time.

I'm reminded of a young student at the university who found himself trapped in a treadmill existence toward nowhere. He approached his English professor and told him why he hadn't been coming to class in recent weeks. He explained that he had been trying to "get his head together" because he didn't "know who he was."

The professor replied, "Well, I know who you are. You're Max Brown, one of my students."

Stunned by the complete absence of sympathy for his position, and placed in this defensive posture, the young man stammered in his own defense, "Yes, I know my name, but I don't know where I am in life."

The teacher answered, "Max, you're in my English class."

Thoroughly rattled and confused now, the student said, "Yes, professor, but I don't know how I'm doing."

His teacher replied, "Max, you're not doing well at all. You're failing English." Life is like that when there is no substantial purpose to live for.

Some people's lives are small because their goals are small. I know a fellow whose main goal in life seems to be to keep the students of a nearby college from cutting across his yard. It torments him to see someone take a shortcut across his yard. First, he put up a string fence. But it didn't work. Then he put up a strand of wire. And that didn't work. Finally, he put up a chain link fence from the corner of his house to the corner of the street. It looks weird, but it works. And his life's goal seems to have been accomplished.

Another man gets totally exercised over his car getting splashed with water or mud. He spends dozens of hours washing his car or driving around looking for parking spaces in out-of-the-way places to avoid splashes.

These folks reveal, by their compulsive behavior over trivial matters, that their purposes for living are trivial, too. You can often tell by what upsets people how big their goals are.

JUDGED BY YOUR AIMS

Those things at which we aim or fail to aim speak volumes about us. Share your goals and aspirations in life, and others can evaluate your character and predict your destiny with a reasonable degree of accuracy.

Actually, it's hard not to tell others your goals because, like that fence the man built, they have a way of sticking out like a sore thumb.

James and John were the sons of Zebedee. One day they approached Jesus and asked him to give them the two top positions in his kingdom. One wanted to sit at his right hand and the other to sit at his left hand. Commenting on this obvious bold ambition to grab the positions of prestige and power in Jesus' kingdom, Cole has written, "The Lord, as usual, allows men to display their own spiritual depth or shallowness by disclosing their aims; for it is by his aims, rather than by his achievements, that a man stands judged."

Goals are obvious. And in dealing with the many couples of clients that I see in counseling, it's obvious that most folks don't have any. At least, they don't have specific, planned out, written down goals. Rare is the couple who have a written will. Rarer still is the couple who have a written one-year or five-year plan for their marriage or family. They talk about planning for the future. They talk about starting a college education fund for their kids. They discuss the need for getting back into activity with the church. But it's soon forgotten because the plan is not concrete and specific. Their goal is to do nothing about goals, and they hit it every time.

When people come to me for counseling, one of the first questions I ask is, "What are your goals, aims and ambitions in life?" Most people do not really know what they are, and those who do often speak in broad general terms. It is obvious that little thought or planning has gone into the selection of a life's goal. It should be embarrassing to stop someone to ask directions, but when they ask you where you're going, you don't know! Such a waste—building roads that lead to nowhere.

No business could survive by charting a course to nowhere. A company without definite purposes and plans for the future will have no future. William James, the noted Harvard psychologist, has written, "There is no more miserable human being than one in whom nothing is habitual but indecision. When you have to make a choice and don't make it, that is in itself a choice."

There was an old woodsman who was known for his sharpshooting ability. He always seemed to hit the bull's-eye. One day a passerby asked how he was so uncannily accurate. He replied, after spitting some tobacco, "Well, young man, I just shoot out into the woods, and if my bullet hits a tree, then I go up and draw a circle around the hole."

That is sometimes our temptation. Having received little instruction or training in the all-important task of formulating and fulfilling specific plans for our lives, we have a tendency to draw a circle of resigned acceptance around whatever we happen to stumble up against in life. Not knowing where we want to go in life or why, most of us are like the proverbial man who jumped on his horse and rode off in all directions. Wall Street ad agents love to dupe these people. They are pushovers for the latest fad merchandising that promises to make them the "envy of their neighborhood." After they are "the first on their block to . . ." buy a fancy new car or put in a swimming pool shaped like a tennis racket, they still feel empty, hollow. So they turn to other fads and empty promises, and the rat race continues.

A NEW NAME FOR AN OLD CONDITION

If my personal observations are correct, most of the students on our university campuses today are looking for more from life than security, comfort and luxury. Most of all, I think they are searching for something to give meaning and significance to life. I believe the present generation of American youth is one of the finest our country has ever produced. They are better developed in body and better trained in mind than my own generation. But on the whole they lack one great essential. Most of them seem to have no high, compelling purpose. They seem to have found no "holy grail" worthy to pursue. They have, essentially, lost touch with life as God intended it to be lived. Thus, a new word, "anomie," has crept into our English dictionaries to identify this condition. This term describes a loss of the sense of who we are. It suggests dangling, no sense of purpose, scattered, unattached, no roots, adrift.

Actually, anomie is simply a new name for an old human condition. And Jesus responded to this undecided or "scattered" condition when he said: "No one can serve two masters" (Matthew 6:24). Elijah confronted the problem when he said to the nation of Israel, "How long will you waver between two opinions? If the Lord is God, follow him, but if Baal is God, follow him" (1 Kings 18:21). Joshua faced the problem on another occasion when he said, "Choose for yourselves this day whom you will serve" (Joshua 24:15).

Peter also addressed the issue in the first gospel sermon. Urging people to follow Jesus — to make him the center of their purposes — he said, "Save yourselves from this *untoward* generation" (Acts 2:40, *KJV*). Untoward — that's an unusual word. It literally means "not going toward anything." Many folks are living an *untoward* life — no direction, no purpose, no meaning. They're running on a treadmill. They're going fast, going often, but going nowhere. They're making a living, but not making a life. They're working for a paycheck, but finding little meaning in their work.

THE UNSTRUCTURED LIFE

Some folks think it's healthy to drift through life without a set plan. They just "go with the flow." They try to relax and just enjoy the trip. These "drifters" are generally living at someone else's expense. No great feat was ever accomplished without great cost. America did not obtain its freedom without bloodshed, for instance.

One psychiatrist points out the hazards of the directionless life with these words: "I consider it a dangerous misconception of mental hygiene to assume that what man needs . . . is equilibrium or homeostasis, a tensionless state. What man actually needs is . . . the striving and struggling for some goal worthy of him" (Frankl, *Search for Meaning*, p. 166).

Recently, I came across some lecture notes in which I had written a statement concerning the advantages of the structured life in comparison with the non-structured life. The statement read: "The ordered, prioritized life is lived with much less stress because it proceeds step by step. Progression and accomplishment are its traits. The disordered life is lived in fits, jerks, repeats, omissions, relapses and hesitations. How can you say, 'It is finished,' if you don't know what you are doing?"

The unstructured life — life without any clearly defined goals, aims and purposes — reminds me of a car I once read about in the newspaper. It seems that the driver pushed the gearshift into "park," pressed down his left foot on the emergency brake, climbed out of the car and left its motor running. While he was gone, the unattended vehicle slipped out of park and fell into reverse. The sudden jerk and movement of the car unlocked the emergency brake, and the vehicle started backing around in circles at 30 miles per hour. The police were called and arrived on the scene. They decided to just keep everyone away from the driverless car until it ran out of gas.

Tragically, many people are living that way. They are going around in circles, going fast but going nowhere. They just keep traveling in the same old ruts until, finally, they run out of gas.

In fact, the whole world at times seems to be operating by this principle. Sometimes there are as many as 40 wars and skirmishes going on in the world at one time. Why this mindless, useless and purposeless destruction of property and human life? I know of only one answer: men are out of control and going nowhere because they will not permit God to order, structure and prioritize their lives. May our constant prayer be, "Your will be done on earth as it is in heaven" (Matthew 6:10). God wants to save us, not only from our sins, but also from a scattered and aimless existence which hurts us and destroys peace on earth and goodwill among men.

HOW IMPORTANT ARE GOALS?

Why do we need to find meaning, direction and purpose in life? Dr. Viktor Frankl, in *Man's Search for Meaning,* describes the terrible suffering in Hitler's concentration camps. He shows how prisoners could endure the most brutal treatment as long as they were clinging to a real purpose for living. Living to finish writing a book, or to rear an abandoned nephew—almost any worthwhile goal—would cause one to fight for survival. A man could stand almost any *what,* if he had a *why.*

What is your supreme aim in life? Is it worth spending yourself on? Paul lists some goals worth setting our sights on. He says, "Aim at righteousness, godliness, faith, love, peace" (2 Timothy 2:12). If you are looking for some challenging goals that will stretch your soul and put spiritual muscles on every fiber and tendon of your being, devote your life to one or all of these goals. And if the time should come when these cease to be a challenge to you, try this one: "Aim at perfection" (2 Corinthians 13:11). That should keep you busy!

What one goal in life does he consider to be most urgent for our personal lives? Listen: "Seek first his kingdom and his righteousness" (Matthew 6:33). To submit to the rule of

God . . . to be right and to do right . . . to glorify him in all that we do . . . to simply live God's way. It is through our pursuit of these goals that life becomes meaningful to us.

QUEST FOR EXCELLENCE

The message of the Bible seems to be: life itself must be centered around the quest for worthwhile ambitions. Zero in on the unique contribution you can make to the glory of God and the good of men. Define it. Plan it. Devote yourself to it. Work at it. Persevere in it.

A sociology professor with an Italian heritage, when telling how he grew up, remarked, "When I would start off to school in the morning, my mother would push the screen door open and call out, "Do you have your lunch pail?" Like all good Italian mothers, his mother made sure he never went hungry.

He said a Jewish boy lived a few doors down. And when he started off to school his mother would push the door open and call out, "Isaac, do you have your books?"

Food or books? It's an interesting contrast of priorities in two distinct ethnic cultures. Italians are devoted to food, and Jews are devoted to learning. In a world of bigotry and anti-Semitism, the Jewish people have risen to top positions in the professions and commercial enterprises in disproportionate numbers because, on the whole, they have definite objectives and relentless determination.

WITH GOALS COME POWER

Ralph Waldo Emerson once said that the power of the Gulf Stream will flow through an ordinary drinking straw, if the straw is placed parallel to the flow of the stream. The same is true of our lives. If we are lined up with God's purposes, if our plans have been conceived in his presence, then his power flows through us as we persevere in the doing of it.

Goals help to focus our lives by concentrating efforts in a specific direction. It reminds me of the focused power of light that has been harnessed as a laser beam. Unlike normal beams of light that scatter their light delicately around a room, the laser beam is so focused that it can hit a four-foot target as far away as the moon with precise accuracy. It can cut a hole through a sheet of steel because its power is concentrated and focused.

When you parallel your life with the power of God, that power will flow through you in amazing ways. You will surprise yourself and others at what you can do. "Now to him who is able to do immeasurably more than all we ask or imagine, according to his power that is at work within us, to him be glory in the church and in Christ Jesus throughout all generations, for ever and ever" (Ephesians 3:20)! "For God did not give us a spirit of timidity, but a spirit of power, of love and of self-discipline" (2 Timothy 1:7).

Gleam In Your Eye

Moses was a meek, unassuming man until God put a gleam in his eye to accomplish the impossible goal of delivering his people from bondage in Egypt. When he first informed Moses of this plan for his life, Moses thought he was inadequate for the task. But God convinced Moses that he would give him all the power he needed; then Moses persevered with a gleam of relentless determination in his eye. In a single-minded commitment to the purpose of freeing his people from slavery, Moses stood before Pharaoh, the powerful king of Egypt, and unflinchingly demanded, "Let my people go!"

Pharaoh replied, "No."

So God exercised his power through Moses to pollute the drinking water in Egypt by saturating it with blood and the stench of decayed and rotting fish. Persevering in his plan, Moses appeared before Pharaoh the second time and demanded, "Let my people go."

Again Pharaoh responded, "No." Can't you see that gleam in his eye when Moses said again, "Let my people go"?

The plague of blood is followed by plagues of frogs, flies, livestock disease, boils, hail, locust and, finally, the plague of death of every firstborn son in Egypt. Now, Pharaoh has had enough! He is eager to let the Israelites go! He is ready to *drive* them out of the land!

Moses delivered over 2 million people out of bondage because he was unstoppable with that gleam of his goal in his eye. Do you have a gleam in your eye?

Under hypnosis or mono-deism (intense concentration on a single idea) you can do all sorts of things that you are usually unable to do when your mind is unfocused. Under hypnosis the human body has amazing abilities. In China major surgery, such as abdominal surgery, is done with no anesthesia—just hypnosis. The human brain, when focused, has amazing properties. Your brain is the same! Only very low intelligence disallows the human brain to focus.

Charles Garfield and his associates at the University of California School of Medicine interviewed 500 high achievers. They concluded: "The single most powerful predictor of success in the long run is commitment—a passion to pursue well-defined goals."

Arie Kieve, a psychiatrist, has written, "Observing the lives of people who have mastered adversity, I have repeatedly noted that they have established goals and, irrespective of obstacles, sought with all their effort to achieve them. From the moment they fixed an objective in their minds and decided to concentrate all their energies on a specific goal, they began to surmount the most difficult odds."

DIVIDED GOALS, DIVIDED POWER

Divided goals mean divided powers. Devote yourself to the doing of 101 good things, and very soon you will lack the ability to do any one of those things exceptionally well.

Focus your mind and body on doing a single task and notice how that tired feeling that weakens your body and drags you down is replaced by a sudden surge of vigor and power.

There's an old adage that says, "If it's worth doing, it's worth doing right." I don't believe it! I can think of a hundred things that have to be done, but they're not worth the concentration to do them extremely well so I can concentrate on doing a few things well. I have to sharpen my pencil to keep writing this manuscript, but I don't need to concentrate on getting "the perfect point" on that pencil in order to continue my work.

My good friend, Dub Orr, said to me recently, "Paul, if you're going to write, you'll have to let the grass grow long." He knows how much I like to keep a neat yard and take care of my 80 rose bushes. But the grass is long, and the fungus has my roses because I'm getting this book finished.

The Single-Eyed Approach

Anything worthwhile takes time away from other projects. The world considers focused effort on one thing fanaticism. That's why some guys are called football fanatics — they can't think about anything else. But the biblical concept is just the opposite. It's a single-eyed view. "Therefore, prepare your minds for action; be self-controlled; *set your hope* [focus your attention] on the grace to be given you when Jesus Christ is revealed" (1 Peter 1:13).

When Jesus suggests the need to have a single-eyed approach to life in Matthew 6:22, he's not saying you should become some kind of physical Cyclops with one giant eyeball in the middle of your forehead. He's simply showing you the need to bring your two eyes into focus. The metaphor suggests that you're cross-eyed when you have one eye on God and the other on the pleasures of the world. "No one can serve two masters."

You have to discipline yourself to reach your goals. To become a great concert pianist, Van Clyburn submitted to the discipline of rigorous practice years on end. I shall never forget the concert where I saw him play with a splint on one finger. Olympic decathlon winners have always been disciplined athletes, observing demanding schedules of exercise and physical exertion. Einstein disciplined himself to sleep only limited amounts of time in order to concentrate on his work. Greatness is a product of goals being pursued and attained through self-discipline, without exception. It is the discipline that brings the aspirations into focus and makes them a reality.

Dick Stuart, one of the nation's foremost marriage therapists, had a personal goal to be a great father. And he was dedicated to it as much as any man I've ever known. Every day he came home early from the office and spent from 4:30 to 8:00 exclusively with his children. It was a time of sharing and learning. Can you imagine how many other things Dick had to say "No" to in order to keep this commitment?

He taught his two-year-old how to play chess! You know how he did it? He first taught the two-year-old what the pawn could do—nothing else, just the pawn. And they only played with the pawns until that one was understood. Then, he taught him what the knight could do, and they just played with the pawns and knights. Finally, the two-year-old understood all the pieces and what they could do. Dick was determined to teach his children, share with them and be with them. But he understood that it took time away from other projects to be a great father.

Have you ever heard of Laffit Pincay, the winning jockey at the Belmont Stakes in 1984? I once overheard a group of men discussing Pincay's abilities. One of them said, "Don't ever bet your money against that fellow." It seems that Pincay was sitting next to him in the first-class section of an airplane once when a fine dinner was served. He said, "The only thing he even touched on his plate was a sack of peanuts. He opened the cellophane wrapper, took out a single peanut and set it on his tray. Then he took his knife, cut the peanut in two and ate one-half of it." Now, even a non-gambler like me had no trouble understanding why you shouldn't wager your money against a disciplined guy like that. Pincay knows he must exercise self-discipline to keep his weight down, and he realizes he must be strong enough to manage and control a 1,500 pound animal in a racing situation. Apparently, his efforts at self-discipline are still paying off. I noticed in the sports section of the newspaper that Laffit Pincay won a million-dollar race at the Santa Anita Handicap riding a horse named Grienton.

Want to win at the game of life? Paul puts the thought in these words: "Endure hardship with us like a good soldier of Christ Jesus. No one serving as a soldier gets involved in civilian affairs—he wants to please his commanding officer. Similarly, if anyone competes as an athlete, he does not receive the victor's crown unless he competes according to the rules. The hardworking farmer should be the first to receive a share of the crops" (2 Timothy 2:3-7).

Notice how many times in these verses Paul refers to the concept of discipline and the rewards of discipline. He talks about hardship, soldiers, athletes, the victor's crown, rules, the hard-working farmer and his share of the crops. All these things require self-control, hard work and discipline. They require focusing attention on one goal and concentrating your efforts until you reach that goal. Then, and only then, does the reward come. Only the soldier who concentrates on being a soldier pleases his commanding officer. Only an athlete who follows the rules wins the victor's crown. And only the farmer who works hard will receive his share of the crops. That's just how life is, folks!

GOALS BRING HARMONY

There's nothing more beautiful to me than sweet, close harmony. And there's nothing more disturbing than discord. Goals bring harmony to your life.

Musicians sometimes write music that contains a dissonance. You have two notes that are right next to each other, and when you hear them clash you say, "Ooooh, that hurts." And when that chord resolves back into sweet harmony, you say, "Ahhhhhh. That's nice."

Discord is the feeling you get when somebody runs their fingernail across a blackboard and cold chills run up your spine. It's grating and uncomfortable.

At our house, if you're standing in the hallway, sometimes you'll have a good case of dissonance or discord. See, I have good music playing in my bedroom on the stereo. (The kids call it "elevator music.") But you'll hear something (I'm not always sure what) very different coming from the stereo in the other bedroom. As long as you're in one or the other bedroom, you're okay. But if you stand in the hall between the two bedrooms you are going to get discord. I guarantee it.

And your life can feel that way, too. You feel discord in your life when you're allowing yourself to be pulled in too many directions at once. When you feel like you've been pulled off course, it's disconcerting. When you feel like you're not making progress toward your ultimate goal, it grates on your nerves, like an unresolved chord.

The pull to get off course is not just between good and bad; sometimes it's between *good and good*. For instance, how should I personally glorify God today? Should I use today to study God's word or go out and share what I already know with someone else? Perhaps I should go work in the church benevolent center today, or should I go visit at the hospital? Which of the hundreds of things I can do to glorify God should I do first? I can't do them all, so I have to choose. I have to set priorities and goals, and then decide what to do on that basis.

Paul knew that we Christians would be wrestling with this tough problem of priorities day by day. He knew, too, that its only adequate solution would be found in the wisdom and power of God. Therefore, we find him praying in our behalf: "It is my prayer that your love may be more and more rich in knowledge and all manner of insight, enabling you to have a sense of what is vital" (Philippians 1:9).

GOALS BRING SIMPLICITY

You have to figure out where you're going. Once you do that and have determined your destination, everything else is simple. If you decide you're going from Washington, D.C., to New York City, then you know what to do to get there. You don't have to worry about Miami or Dallas or Los Angeles anymore. They have no relevance to your destination. You won't be pulled in all those different directions anymore because they just don't fit in with your goal.

Few men in recent history have influenced the lives of millions like Ghandi of India. His goals were simple, and his life-style was simple. How can you explain the power and the influence possessed by this man, not only in his own country, but throughout the world? By concentrating and focusing his mind and body on one thing, and by persevering toward his goal with discipline, he reaped the power and rewards of his single-minded efforts.

Thoreau, the poet-philosopher said, "Let your matters be as one or two." Thoreau's life-style was so simple that he lived on 37 cents a week. It's easy to see that he was not a man mastered by his possessions. By not expending his mind and energy on the accumulation of things, he was able to pursue the goals that were vital to him with greater concentration and power.

Incidentally, did you know there are a lot of people in America today *voluntarily* living on $3,000 a year or less? It's voluntary poverty. They don't take it from the government; they earn it. The Quakers and others are doing just that. They live more simply because they have a different dream than the typical American dream of a lot of stuff and junk.

When Jesus died, he didn't have a very big wardrobe. In fact, he only had one possession for which the Roman soldiers were willing to roll their dice—that one seamless robe. He lived a simple, goal-directed life.

WHAT AM I TO BE ABOUT?

How should I select goals and priorities for my life? God didn't create us as a mass of robots but as intelligent, distinctive and creative individuals with a purpose and endowed with special gifts. God has as many unique plans as he has unique people. No detail of heredity or environment, of temperament or talent is left out. He has uniquely equipped you for some special task in the accomplishment of *his* purposes. The acceptance of this challenge is intensely personal.

The Bible says, "If you cry out for insight and raise your voice for understanding, if you seek it like silver and search for it as for hidden treasure; then you will understand the fear of the Lord and find the knowledge of God. For the Lord gives wisdom; from his mouth come knowledge and understanding" (Proverbs 2:3-6).

God Bless The Turtles

It's kind of like the story about the race between the rabbit and the turtle. The old jackrabbit had a high IQ of the legs. He could just run like mad. The old turtle had been short-changed in the legs, and even his running style was more of a creep than a crawl. But he could plod and persevere and was disciplined and determined enough to do just that.

When the race began, the jackrabbit leaped out from the starting blocks, kicked dust in the face of his competitor and soon left the turtle so far behind him that he decided to stop for a bit to relax. He'd run awhile and rest awhile, run awhile and rest awhile. But the old turtle just kept plodding along the course until he passed the napping rabbit near the finish line and won the race.

God bless the turtles! The church, as you know, gets its work done with volunteer labor. And this means that when there's a specific job to do, you've got to use those animals whom you can find and who are willing to accept the harness. The ten-talent jackrabbits can cover a lot of territory and get a lot done in a hurry. But they are hard to find, and when you do find them they are usually so wrapped up in other activities that they are reluctant to accept the bridle. If it weren't for the turtles who accept those unglamorous jobs that consume your time and tie you down for long periods of time, not much work in the church would ever get done. If anyone in the church deserves to be honored, it is those disciplined turtles who are determined to persevere until the task is completed.

Whatever your gifts or gift may be, just give it to the Lord and let him use it to accomplish his purposes and plans. Try to visualize a 55-gallon oil barrel in front of you with a tiny thimble resting on the ground beside it. That 55-gallon barrel is jam-packed with the unique gifts and talents that God bestowed on Paul, the apostle, and that tiny little thimble is jam-packed with the gifts and talents that God has given to Paul, the Faulkner.

My gift from God, you see, is to be a thimble. And someone says, "But wouldn't you rather be a barrel like the apostle Paul?" Well, I don't know about that. There's just not enough metal in me to make a 55-gallon barrel, and if you tried to stretch me that far, it would destroy me, and I could no longer function as a thimble.

You say, "But that's not fair."

Of course, it's fair. The Lord needs thimbles! The Lord made me a thimble because he needs and uses thimbles as well as he makes, needs and uses barrels.

Some of my earliest childhood memories center around my mother's unorthodox use of a common, metal sewing thimble. She did a lot of sewing on an old treadle machine. I liked to gather up my toys and books and entertain myself around, and sometimes beneath, Mama's feet. When I would bump into the foot operated treadle and mess up Mama's sewing or do something else that I shouldn't be doing, she would take that metal thimble and thump me on the head with it. Have you ever been disciplined on the top of the head with a metal thimble? Believe me, she could raise a knot with that thing! But if she had hit me on the head with a 55-ballon barrel, she'd have killed me!

There are some things that you can do with a thimble that you can't do with a barrel. A barrel is great for storing and shipping oil, but it does not make a very good sewing implement. If you're a thimble, don't try to make your thimble into a barrel. Or, if you're a barrel, don't try to be a water-tower tank or a 5-gallon bucket. The Lord needs barrels, too. He needs and uses us all.

IT IS FINISHED

A student of mine was a conscientious objector during the time of the war in Vietnam. Agreeing to serve his country in a non-violent capacity, the government assigned him to work as an orderly in Scott and White Hospital of Temple, Texas. He told me of an interesting incident that happened in the intensive care unit of the hospital late one night.

An old man was a patient in the intensive care unit, and there seemed to be little hope that he could regain his health. He had lost his first wife through death and had married a much younger woman who was interested not so much in him as in his money. While he was in the hospital, his second wife filed for divorce and was suing him for everything she could get. Because he was old and dying, he didn't much care who got his money. He'd just let her have it without going through the hassles of a legal battle.

In the middle of the night, the old man nearly died from a ruptured blood vessel. Although there were no doctors on duty at that late hour, a quick-thinking nurse handled the situation in the correct manner and saved the old man's life.

A few hours later, the old man looked up at the nurse and said to her in a very weak and feeble voice of appreciation, "You saved my life."

The nurse replied, "No, I didn't save your life. God did. Now it's up to you to find out why."

When the old man recovered, he had a new goal and purpose in life. He decided that he was going to start doing some good things for people that he should have been doing all along. He contested his divorce and kept his money, not to lavish things upon himself but to be generous, kind and helpful to people. The student told me about the remarkable transformation that occurred in the old man's life as he became aware of those things in life that are most important and vital.

At age 12 Jesus had a compelling plan and purpose for his life. What did Jesus consider to be most vital for his own unique and distinctive life? He replies, "I must be about my father's business." Doing God's work. That was Jesus' goal from the age of 12 until he whispered with his last breaths of life from the cross, "It is finished." Was it really? Were all the sick folks healed? Were all the hungry people fed? Did he mean that there was no more work that God wanted to be done? No. But what he came to do, he did. *It* was finished.

And what about when it's your turn to go? What if the garage hasn't been cleaned out? And what if there's still stuff under the bed? What if the flowerbed hasn't been weeded and the roses need spraying? So, who cares? If what you came to do, you did, then you can say, "It's finished." You must learn to say, "I came to do my father's will." And then do it!

You can't hook yesterday's plowing to today's plow.

Forgetting what is behind and straining toward what is ahead, I press on toward the goal to win the prize for which God has called me heavenward in Christ Jesus.

— Philippians 3:13-14

CHAPTER FIVE

Don't Kill Today with Yesterday

When Thomas Carlyle had finished writing his history of the French Revolution, he took the manuscript to a neighbor, John Stuart Mill, for proofreading. A few days later, Mill came to Carlyle's house with disastrous news. His maid had used the manuscript to start a fire in the fireplace.

Carlyle raged like a madman for several days. For two full years he had poured his whole being into that manuscript. Now, it was gone. Two years of his life were reduced to ashes. In view of that tragic blunder, Carlyle thought he could never again give himself to the difficult discipline of writing.

One day Carlyle stood looking out his second story window over the rooftops near his home. Across the way he saw a stone mason slowly and patiently rebuilding a collapsed wall, putting one stone upon another, until finally the new wall took form. For the first time Carlyle accepted the unfortunate mistake of his past and began to rewrite his book. Diligently, one page at a time, one day at a time, he wrote and finished what was probably his finest work.

To make things right when they go wrong in your life, you must rebuild by carefully replacing one stone of your life upon another, one day at a time.

HOW CAN I FORGIVE MYSELF?

Ralph Waldo Emerson's daughter was away from home attending school. In corresponding with her famous father, she had made it clear to him that she was brooding over a past mistake that had left her with a troubled conscience. Emerson wrote his daughter and said:

> Finish every day and be done with it. You have done what you could. Some blunders and absurdities no doubt crept in; but get rid of them and forget them as soon as you can. Tomorrow is a new day, and you should never encumber its potentialities and invitations with the dread of the past. You should not waste a moment of today on the rottenness of yesterday.

Maybe you, too, are living with a sense of failure and guilt, an unhappy realization that you haven't been the kind of person you ought to be. Maybe your marriage is on the rocks because of past blunders and failures. How can you get over your failures? How can you forgive yourself and begin again?

A young woman says, "I'm a murderer. I got pregnant out of wedlock. My parents insisted that I get an abortion. They seemed concerned only over the fact that there might be a scandal. I felt terribly guilty about the idea of taking the life being formed in me; but my parents insisted, so I had the abortion. How can I forgive myself?"

A young man says, "My father died last year. Before he died, we had a heated quarrel; and I said some cruel and hostile things. I made no effort to reconcile our differences. How can I forgive myself?"

A middle-aged man says, "I neglected to give my children the care and attention they needed in their formative years. Their behavior as adults is proof of my failure as a father. How can I forgive myself?"

COMING TO GRIPS WITH THE PAST

Perhaps you've observed that some people have stumbled and failed times without number. Yet, they are able to come to grips with the past and move ahead with the living of today with greater zest and vigor than ever before. How do they do it? How can you do it?

You would do well to talk to yourself about the past. You need to say: "Self, the past is gone. There is nothing you can do to change it. So why waste your strength wrestling with the past when you need all your power to grapple with the vital issues of today."

In the closing scene of Shakespeare's *The Tempest*, Prospero says of Alonzo: "Let us not burden our remembrances with a heaviness that's gone." Vivien Larrimore gives similar advice in her poem, *Keys*.

> I've shut the door on yesterday
> Its sorrow and mistakes:
> And now I throw the key away to seek another room
> And furnish it with hope and smiles
> And every springtime bloom.
> I've shut the door on yesterday
> And thrown the key away.
> Tomorrow holds no fears for me,
> Since I have found today.

It's foolish to cling to unresolved problems and difficulties from the past and to bring the burdens and worries about the future into today's schedule. Our shoulders are just not broad or strong enough to carry the loads of more than one day, and only then by the grace of God.

ONE LOAD AT A TIME

In Texas, we have a lot of pick-up trucks. They're as much a part of our culture as are gunracks, cowboy hats and big belt buckles. What would happen to a pick-up truck if you placed on it all the loads it had ever carried in the past? It would break it down! The same thing would happen if you tried to put on it all the loads it would ever carry in the future. That pick-up would simply collapse under the burden. It was designed to carry one load at a time. And it will serve you well, if you use it that way—one load at a time.

Only today is ours—a gift from the Almighty—and he promises to provide us with the strength to live it. He doesn't promise to give us strength and endurance for yesterday's contests. He promises his strength, just for today. "As thy days, so shall thy strength be" (Deuteronomy 33:25).

As in Old Testament times when God fed his people daily with manna, so shall he supply his grace now. They could not store up the manna for a rainy day because God wanted them to depend on him daily. God always seems to work that way. He doesn't teach us to pray for tomorrow's wants but for today's needs. "Give us this day, our *daily* bread." He doesn't give his power in advance, lest we rely on ourselves and not in him alone. He promises strength, just for today. "As thy days, so shall thy strength be."

Jesus warns about bringing tomorrow and its anticipated problems into today's schedule. "Therefore, do not worry about tomorrow for tomorrow will worry about itself. Each day has enough trouble of its own" (Matthew 6:34).

So let's live today in the strength of God. Don't borrow yesterday's troubles and tomorrow's problems because they will consume your strength for enjoying today. Today well-lived will make every yesterday a dream of happiness and tomorrow a vision of hope.

Sybil Partridge said it this way: "So for tomorrow and its needs, I do not pray; but keep me, guide me, love me, Lord, just for today."

ONE DAY AT A TIME

The members of Alcoholics Anonymous have a slogan that says: "I can make it, *one day at a time*." And that's the only way they do make it. Don't tell an alcoholic to not take a drink for the next nine months. It's too much of an overload. He will break under the impossible thought. But if you encourage him not to take a drink today — *just* today — that's a possibility! "I can make it, one day at a time."

God's power comes as you yield your will to his will — one day at a time. "*This* is the day which the Lord hath made; we will rejoice and be glad in it" (Psalm 118:24, *KJV*).

Jesus makes it clear: "No one who puts his hand to the plow and looks back is fit for service in the kingdom of God" (Matthew 9:62). Why? If you take your eyes off the things God wants you to do today to look over your shoulder at the headache of your past, it makes you unfit for kingdom service today.

Farmers understand it well. They say, "You can't hook yesterday's plowing to today's plow." Simple. It reminds me of the positive words from the apostle Paul: "One thing I do: Forgetting what is behind and straining toward what is ahead, I press on toward the goal to win the prize for which God has called me heavenward in Christ Jesus" (Philippians 3:13,14). "*One* thing I do." Oh my, that already helps, doesn't it? I've been trying to do a dozen things all at once. How about you? What a great message for today's harem-scarem world! Just do *one* thing.

Well, Paul was a specialist. He never diffused his talents and power by giving himself to a dozen different tasks. He didn't even take on two. He gave all his time, attention, abilities and strength to a single task. "*One* thing I do."

You see, life becomes powerful and successful only as its powers are focused. Give yourself equally to a large number of tasks, and soon each of them will begin to suffer. It's the familiar cry of "too many irons in the fire" and "spreading yourself too thin." Instead of saying, "This one thing I do," do you often have to say, "These dozen things I dabble in"? Learn to concentrate your efforts doing one thing well, and there's no telling how far you can go or how successful you can become.

FORGET WHAT IS BEHIND

Above all, the apostle says, you need to forget what is behind and strain toward what is ahead. The word *forgetting* is a key word. Please keep in mind that in biblical terminology, "forgetting" rarely means the inability to remember. Apart from senility, hypnosis or a brain malfunction, few normal folks can forget what's happened in their past. The biblical meaning of forgetting is "no longer being influenced or affected by something."

So, when Paul urges you to forget what is behind, he is not suggesting that you remove all memories of the past from your mind. He simply wants you no longer to be influenced by those memories of the past which could hinder your efforts to strain toward what is ahead." Paul's message is this: "Don't let yesterday's mistakes paralyze today's efforts and hinder tomorrow's achievements. Stop living in the past!"

As hard as we may try, we can live only one day at a time, and that day is always today. Yesterday is past, irrevocably and irretrievably gone. We cannot walk back into it or lay any new claim upon it. And the future belongs to us no more than the past. We may prepare and plan for the future, but we will never be able to live in it. For when it arrives, it becomes the now of today. Live today!

PROBLEMS WITH LIVING IN THE PAST!

A Technical Impossibility

Physically, you can't live in the past. It is a technical impossibility. Your body exists in the present. You can't back up even one second. You are locked into a time capsule which drags you through life to death. You can fight or cooperate with "father time," but you cannot change it. You don't function well when your body is standing at home plate while your mind is wandering around somewhere out in left field. In order to play the ballgame of life in the present, your mind must be focused on the curve ball that was just thrown lickety split by the pitcher.

Even in the design of your body, God makes it clear that he never intended for your mind to dwell very long on the past. He pointed your face toward the future and makes it difficult for you to glance over your shoulders at what lies behind. He put eyes in the front of your head, not in the back. He made your hands, not to wrestle with the problems and mistakes behind you, but to grapple with the tasks before you. He designed your feet for moving forward, not backward. Even the design of your body bears witness to God's silent message of "don't look back, but strain forward."

One old couple fussed and fought all the time. Finally, they solved their problem by setting a date. They chose the date July 6, 1976. They decided that if something happened before that date they weren't going to talk about it. Well, guess what. That killed almost all their fussing because most of their disagreements centered around some unfinished "junk" that had never been straightened out pre-1976.

What a great idea! You can set the date for not remembering as yesterday, if you wish. It makes a lot of sense. You can't do anything about it, so why rehash it and get upset about it all over again. Start from today, and go forward.

Past Memories Are Flawed

Another reason you shouldn't look very long at the past is because your memories are faulty. Researchers have traced accounts given in counseling sessions. They have documented the events told in many counseling sessions as the client recalled them. Over and over again, after checking with parents, neighbors, relatives, friends and school authorities, the events either never happened or were grossly misunderstood. This is the norm.

It's like two people standing on opposite sides of the same intersection recalling an automobile accident they both witnessed. Each one gives a different account of the incident. Why? Their perspectives are different. They remember the incident differently because memories are faulty.

If, indeed, our memories are given to such private interpretation, we must then be extremely careful about judging ourselves of others by our memories of how things were.

Idealizing the Good Ol' Days

Have you ever noticed the glamor and glitter attributed to the "good old days?"

> Pepsi-Cola hits the spot:
> Twelve full ounces — that's a lot.
> Twice as much for a nickel, too.
> Pepsi-Cola is the drink for you.

Are you old enough to remember that jingle? Well, today they are trying to rob me by charging 75 cents for a nickel Pepsi! It's an outrage! I remember when Snicker bars were as big as a quarter-pound of butter and sold for a nickel.

Yes, the old days were good days. Back then, you could drive up to a filling station, get a dollar's worth of gas, and the attendant would vacuum your car, wash the windows inside and out, check the tires, battery, oil, water and even the level of your brake fluid. This morning I drove into a filling station. The guy pumping gas didn't check the oil, didn't clean the windshield, let the gas overflow and then forgot to put the gas cap back on. That's what is so discouraging about *self-service* today. It's always so bad.

No wonder we long for the "good old days" when we glamorize it so — we have forgotten there was no air-conditioning, and we got out of a sweaty bed on hot summer mornings. We have conveniently forgotten when there was no central heating, and we stood in front of those gas heaters on cold winter mornings scorching our backsides while freezing on the front. We've forgotten what it was like to have three rooms and a *path* leading to a wooden lean-to that backed up to the north wind and bathing in a #3 tub, instead of a carpeted room with a padded seat and a hot tub.

Our memories of the "good old days" are faulty. Someone said it like this: "The man who remembers with delight the chocolate pie that grandma used to make has forgotten the indigestion that grandpa used to have."

Your Floppy Disk Gets Full

A couple of years back I bought a computer for word processing. Now, you probably know that a word processor puts words on a screen, just like a typewriter puts them on paper. The difference is that the words are not in indelible ink, so you can change them, move them around, zap them off the screen entirely and a variety of other things. It's a wonderful gadget . . . when it works right.

When you get the words organized and strung together the way you want them into sentences and paragraphs, you can punch a couple of buttons, and the computer will save what you've done. By punching the "Control" key, the "K" and the "B" keys all at once, you command the computer to take the words out of its electronic memory and record them (or save them) on a magnetic disk, sort of like a song put on a record. Then you can retrieve them when you need them later and print them out or rearrange them again.

Well, I was working with it about two o'clock one morning on this very book. I finally got it just like I wanted it and said, "That's great." Proudly I punched the three keys to save the material. Well, the memory whirred a bit, then it went over to the floppy disk to record it permanently. And that whirred a bit. And then a message came up on the screen: "You have committed a fatal error." And all the material disappeared. The computer had wiped out all the pages of outline in its electronic memory and had saved nothing.

I calmly reached over for my wrench that was lying nearby and seethed, "No! *You* are the one who has committed the fatal error!" And I felt like doing to that computer what the Lord did to the fig tree that promised him something it couldn't deliver. But what's the point?

The problem was that I had unknowingly overloaded the floppy disk earlier. It simply couldn't handle any more information. It was full. And when I tried to force it to eat more than it could hold, it malfunctioned. It reminded me of a baby that's had one too many spoons of carrots shoved down its mouth. It simply spit it out.

I wasted about two days of my life fretting over that mistake. Finally, I came to grips with that irritation in the same way you will need to handle yours. I accepted it, learned from it and started over.

The correlation between your mind and body is similar to the one existing between a floppy disk and a computer. Overload the mind with too many burdensome and distressing memories from the past, and your body will begin to malfunction like an overloaded disk. So bring your mind back into the present, and hook it up with your body, which has no choice but to live in the present. Function as God intended for you to function . . . one day at a time. And that day is today.

Two ugly ghosts from the past like to loiter in your mind and overload your body to prevent you from living happily in the present. The first is guilt. The second is resentment. The remainder of this chapter will deal with guilt and how to handle it. Resentment will be discussed in chapter six.

GUILT

Two Kinds of Guilt

There are two kinds of guilt, according to the Swiss psychiatrist, Paul Tournier. In his book, *Guilt and Grace,* he distinguishes between false guilt and true guilt: "False guilt is that which comes as a result of the judgments and suggestions of me. True guilt is that which results from Divine judgment."

There is a kind of guilt which psychological techniques can remove. It falls within the category Tournier defines as false guilt. Childhood memories of naughtiness, anxiety over violation of social customs and offenses against class or society's moral code create guilt. For these feelings of a tender and sensitive conscience, the therapy of wise human counseling may be adequate to make things right when they go wrong.

But what about real guilt, deep guilt? There are some actions which go far beyond offending man's standards; they break universal laws—God's laws. When this happens, your conscience is activated; and you have feelings of true guilt. It puts a blight on your spirit which can shatter personality and is beyond your power to reach. Murder, adultery, lying and pride are just a few of the actions that can produce true guilt, deep guilt within you.

Yet, your guilt before God is more than any specific incident or combination of incidents. It is the knowledge that deep within you is a fatal flaw that cannot be made right by your own effort. Something (someone) greater — much greater — will have to help you overcome psychologically and spiritually. "We have all sinned and fallen short of the glory of God" (Romans 3:23). We are not what we ought to be, and we know it! We feel it. And we fear it.

Unresolved guilt, true or false, is probably the most devastating of all the emotions. It demoralizes your mind with a thousand anxieties and robs your body of strength for living today. Guilt depresses your mind, crushes your spirit and discourages your body from functioning positively and effectively. The result? You feel hopeless, helpless and worthless.

The High Price of Guilt

King David, thousands of years ago, wrote of his personal battle with the problem of unresolved guilt. The problem began for David like many today — with a third party. One day he was walking on the roof of his house, and he saw a very beautiful woman bathing. All he could think about was that he wanted her. Well, he got her. But in the process he not only robbed another man of his wife but also sent the man, Uriah, into the front lines of battle to be killed. Adultery and murder hung over David's head like the deadly blade of a poised guillotine.

Nathan the prophet confronted David with his sin against God, and the king was truly repentant. However, a man learns slowly in life that sooner or later you must sit down to a banquet of consequences for your misdeeds. David was no exception. Nathan announced to him that, as punishment for his sin, the child born to Bathsheba would die. King David knew what it was like to live with the problem of unresolved guilt. You don't steal another man's wife, send him to his death and lose your young son to disease without knowing and feeling the guilt. His poetic way of describing his guilt is recorded in Psalm 32. In verse 3 David describes his physical reaction to the load of guilt: "When I kept silent, my bones wasted away through my groaning all day long."

His nights were no happier. "For day and night your hand was heavy upon me; my strength was sapped as in the heat of summer" (Psalm 32:4). And by verse 5 David had suffered long enough. By listening in on his conversation with

God, we discover how he found freedom from guilt. "Then I acknowledged my sin to you and did not cover up my iniquity. I said, 'I will confess my transgressions to the Lord,' and you forgave the guilt of my sin."

David's joy in resolving the guilt problem is expressed in the introductory lines of this psalm: "Blessed is he whose transgressions are forgiven, whose sins are covered. Blessed is the man whose sin the Lord does not count against him and in whose spirit is no deceit" (Psalm 32:1,2).

Unless you deal decisively with unresolved guilt, it will turn the tables and deal decisively with you. We are not punished *for* our sins as much as we are punished *by* our sins. "He who conceals his sins does not prosper, but whoever confesses and renounces them finds mercy" (Proverbs 28:13).

HOW GUILT WORKS

Whenever you violate your moral values, you create a psychological *debt*. And debts always have to be paid back, one way or another. When you violate another moral code that you hold, more debt is stacked up in your column. Your conscience is the debt collector. It is that part of you that makes you feel guilty. It is often the source that allows your body to create headaches, ulcers and other maladies. It stays after you until the debt is paid. And it never gives up.

The American Indians pictured the conscience as a triangle, a three-cornered stone located deep within your bosom. If you were an Indian, when you violated your values the stone would revolve or turn. With each turn the corners cut you, but the corner wore off a little, too. If you continued violating your conscience, sooner or later you would round off the sharp corners of the stone, and your conscience could no longer "cut" you as it should.

This is an accurate description of the person who is a sociopath or psychopath, whom we will describe later. So when you violate your values, your conscience says, "You've written a hot check on your personal account with God. It's marked *insufficient funds*." You also write hot checks against yourself and others. Essentially, though, all debts are against God's account. If you had not violated *his* will, you would not have created any other debts against yourself or others.

VAIN ATTEMPTS TO PAY OFF DEBTS

The Immature Attempt

Well, how will you pay off your debt? Some folks would answer, "I'll just do enough good things to pay it back." You cannot do enough good deeds to deliver yourself from the guilt of even a single misdeed. It is similar to a man without funds writing a worthless check to satisfy the demands of a $10 million loan. In order to pay debts, you must have a *positive* cash flow. In the Christian sense only Jesus has a positive cash flow. The rest of us are in debt. To "earn" salvation we would have to live better than perfect to have any surplus funds to pay back any debt.

Imagine a man in a court of law. He owes the federal government the sum of $3 million for failing to pay his income tax. The man is stone broke and unable to repay his debt, but he makes an interesting argument in his own defense. He says, "Your honor, it is true that I didn't pay my income tax. But feeling a keen sense of guilt over my failure, I started to do some good things to make up for my failure in this regard. I started obeying, perfectly, all of the other rules and regulations of the government to which I am subject. In view of my present obedience to governmental regulations and rules, I am asking the government to pay me for my good conduct so I can pay off my tax debt with the sum that I've earned."

You see the point, don't you? Will the government cancel his debt because he's started doing a lot of good things he was obligated to do anyway? That which is true in the physical realm is also true in the spiritual realm. Jesus makes it clear that you can't repay your debt to God by doing the things that you ought to have been doing anyway. "So you also, when you have done everything you were told to do, should say, 'We are unworthy servants; we have only done our duty'" (Luke 17:10). You cannot do enough good things to repay your debt to God, but all debts still must be paid.

The Depressive Attempt

Others seek to pay off their debt to God with grief time. They reason, "If I hurt and grieve over my mistakes long enough, my guilt feelings will leave me." This method is chosen by people who are given to depression. They think if they hurt or grieve long enough, their hurt and suffering will be credited against their debt. It's the same way they do the dishes. When they come to a dish that has egg stuck on it that won't come off with minimal scrubbing, they just soak it. If the dish is soaked long enough, the dried egg will soften and wash away. But real sin debts don't just soak off with time. They must be paid in full.

The Neurotic Attempt

Still others say, "Well, I'll just get sick, and that will take care of the problem." They actually don't say, "I'll get sick." It happens almost subconsciously. The body has an uncanny way of picking up on our thinking, haven't you noticed? When you don't *feel* like going to church, your body cooperates by developing a headache, upset stomach or something worse. "And it may get worse," you're thinking. "Better play it safe and stay home."

Our society accepts sickness as an adequate reason to miss work, for instance. You know that if you call in "sick," the boss will probably buy it. But if you call in and say you have "spring fever" or you're "lazy," it just won't fly. So you learn early to play the sick game. Why? Because it works!

Some reports indicate that as many as 50% of the hospital beds are filled with these kinds of folks. They are called *psychosomatic* illnesses. Oh, they're physically ill all right, but the illness was brought on by thinking (consciously or subconsciously) that they could get excused from their debts to society or their jobs by getting sick because, after all, nobody will make a sick person pay his debts. Wrong! Debts must be paid!

The Criminal Attempt

Finally, there are those people who "pass the buck" and deny responsibility for their actions. Included in this group are the sociopaths and criminals. The Nazi war criminal said, "I was just following orders. I didn't really want to exterminate the Jews. Hitler made me do it."

The criminal says, "I'm the product of the neighborhood I was brought up in. Don't blame me; blame the environment."

Thc wife and child abuser says, "My problem is that I was raised by abusive parents. Don't blame me; blame them."

The denial of guilt does not remove it or lessen responsibility for it. It only suppresses guilt by stuffing it into the unconscious regions of our minds. We may think our feelings of guilt are dormant because we've ignored them. But they are not quiet. One day feelings of guilt surge into a conscious level. They manifest themselves in physical and mental illnesses or ugly acts of resentment and cruelty. Our internal conflict always finds a way to express itself; and sadly enough, our ugly actions often hurt the people who love us the most.

Of course, anyone can play the game of denial. It all started in the garden of Eden (Genesis 3:1-19). Adam ate the forbidden fruit, and God called him on the grass carpet. Adam said, "I'm not responsible. The woman you gave me, remember her? Well, she gave me fruit from the tree, and I ate it. Don't blame me; blame her."

Then God asked Eve, "What have you done?"

She said, "The serpent deceived me, and I ate."
But God held them *all* responsible!

BUT HOW DO I FORGIVE MYSELF?

The debts owed to God *cannot* be paid back by any of your own efforts. But, wait! You're not hopeless. And God is not evil because he made you this way. He just wants you to acknowledge, without question, your ineptness, your real weakness at solving your own sin (real guilt) problems. He wants to dynamite your mind loose from grasping power you can never obtain anyway. Thus humbled, you can learn the eternal power of love. It's love that is unearned and unmerited. It's love which was given on the cross at no cost to you but great cost to him. It's the love that paid your debt because debts *must* be paid.

So you can continually rejoice in the spiritual banker who countersigned your note of debt. "Therefore, there is now no condemnation (indebtedness) for those who are in Christ Jesus" (Romans 8:1). God has looked at your spiritual bank balance and declared you debt free. Rejoice!

But you might say, "I can't rejoice. I know God has forgiven me, but I can't forgive myself." The point is, you never could. You just thought you could. You could never pay the debt because it was against God. When he forgives, that's it. Take yourself out of the forgiveness business. You may *feel* guilty (in debt), but that doesn't mean you *are* guilty. That's just pseudo guilt (false guilt). It won't hurt you. it might even keep you humble. But if it lingers, see your minister or counselor. Hopefully, among other things, he will remind you again that the *real* debt has been paid in full, thanks to God! He has made everything right when everything went wrong.

As the words of the song so aptly put it:

> He paid a debt He did not owe;
> I owed a debt I could not pay;
> I needed someone to wash my sins away
> And now I sing a brand new song—amazing grace!
> Christ Jesus paid the debt that I could never pay.

Forgive as freely as the Lord has forgiven you.

— Colossians 3:13, Phillips

It's tough to give up resentment sometimes. With resentment come bitterness and hate — a double-barreled backfire. So, what looks like sacrifice in giving up resentment is really wisdom.

CHAPTER SIX

Cut Your Line When It's Tangled

Have you ever rared back to throw a fishing lure *way out* in the lake, but when you cast, the line just balled up on the reel? And you're standing there looking at that tangled backlash wondering what to do about it.

Your reaction is very important. Most fishermen just snip the line, pull out a new line, rebait the hook and keep on fishing. But others just "can't waste all that good line." So they waste good fishing time, when the fish are biting and the mosquitos aren't, tediously trying to untangle their lines. And, usually, they end up cutting the line anyway.

Two people may experience the same problem, but each uses a different method to come to grips with it. One deals with the problem of a tangled fishing line in a quick and decisive fashion. He cuts away the tangled line, salvages the good line and immediately moves toward the goal of fishing. The other looks at the tangled line and thinks: "I can't do another thing until I get my fishing line untangled."

Do you see the implications of that sort of mind-set? This person may be saying, "I'm going to straighten out this mess, even though it means I will do no more fishing today." Have you ever known folks like that? They get so exercised over the tangled problems of the past that they have no energy left for the business of living today.

When things go wrong, which of these two approaches do you use to make things right?

The Thrill of the Drill

A friend of mine decided to drill a water well. Others living near him had drilled wells and struck water at a depth of 70 feet. My friend drilled down 70 feet. No water. He drilled to 100 feet. No water. He drilled to 200 feet. No water. Three hundred feet. Four hundred feet. Same story. He was headed straight for China!

Finally, he decided to accept his loss, pull out of the hole and drill for water in another location. Was that wise? Should he have determined, "I'm going to drill this hole to the bitter end"? Or did he do the right thing when he decided, "This is obviously a dry hole; it's ridiculous to keep drilling here; it's time to cut the line"?

Some people just like to drill for the thrill of it. They delight in drilling new holes in old wounds and like to uncover old resentments that lie buried in the garbage of the past. The tragedy of dredging up old resentments from the past is that it sours our disposition, shrivels our spirit and makes us miserable while hurting the people around us.

Resentment Defined

Do you know the origin of the word resentment? It comes from the Latin word *resento*, which essentially means to re-feel. Someone may hurt you deeply. Temporarily, you may shove that tragic experience into your subconscious. But then something happens to conjure up that painful memory. And you re-feel the full agony and hurt of it. You may even externalize those feelings by lashing out in anger and resentment at someone else.

Married couples are often specialists in resentment. They probe around in the garbage dump searching for old, sharp bones of contention from the past they can use as weapons to wound one another. They delight in deliberately lashing one another with old mistakes and probing old sores. It's tragic, isn't it? All that resentment and hurt! And there's not one positive thing to be gained by it.

What can you do with resentment? You have to cut the line! You must "forget what lies behind" and "strain toward what lies ahead."

Do you waste a lot of today's energy trying to untangle lines that got tangled in your yesterdays? Trying to straighten out all of those old problems will only breed more resentment. So, why not cut the line and get back to fishing?

When you were a kid, did your mom or grandma have a slop bucket? You know, it sat over in some out-of-sight corner in the old kitchen where the smell couldn't be detected too easily. Sometimes it even had a lid. And every few minutes when she was cooking Grandma would throw something in there that she didn't want to keep — trimmings off the meat, potato peels, spoiled milk and all the rest of the leftover food garbage. I think "slop" was a good name for it.

Then about every two or three days someone would have to take that bucket full of slop and go pour it into the pig's trough. Sometimes that old pig would get so excited about eating he couldn't wait for them to finish pouring, and he'd stick his head under the pouring slop. Well, I've found out that folks carry their own personal slop buckets around with them. Especially married folks do. But these are emotional slop buckets. We fill them up with all our leftover feelings and emotions from spats and quarrels. We throw in the trimmings from old conflicts and disagreements. We just collect all sorts of emotional slop from our past.

Then, every so often, when our emotions are running high over some current problem, we grab up our slop buckets and empty them on the heads of our husband, wife, kids or friends. We pour out all the slop from our past and muck up the present with it. It's disgusting!

Christ Took the Initiative

Let's face it. It's going to take a deep conviction to inspire you to impale yourself on a cross for the privilege of forgiving someone who hates you. Only a compelling love for the One who loved you and gave himself up for you could provide you with the necessary incentive.

That's why we need to think about the unjust agony our Lord willingly took upon himself. His trial was unjust. Pilate knew Jesus had done nothing wrong. His wife had warned him. But he had his soldiers scourge him anyway. Pilate may have been trying to say to the mob, "I've scourged him. Scourging's enough."

But it wasn't enough. A bloodthirsty crowd cried out, "Crucify him! Crucify him!" So he hung on the cross absolutely innocent. And even as his executioners were putting him to death, he cried out (without resentment) for people who had not even requested his forgiveness: "Father, forgive them, for they do not know what they are doing" (Luke 23:34).

Jesus took the initiative to forgive those who never even requested it. He did his part — whether the crowd accepted it or not. Their forgiveness came later when they realized that Jesus had taken the loving initiative and met their hate and resentment with his forgiveness. His anticipating action melted their hearts. In a loving effort to put things right, they asked, "What must we do to be saved" (Acts 2:37)?

While it is true that God rewards only those who request his forgiveness, it is his *intent* to lavish his forgiveness upon every person. He demonstrated this by taking the *initiative* even toward those who never requested it. "You see, at just the right time, when we were still powerless, Christ died for the ungodly . . . But God demonstrates his own love for us in this: While we were still sinners, Christ died for us" (Romans 5:6-8).

So, the Christian concept is this: when people mistreat you, and feelings of resentment arise within you, don't express resentment toward them. Take the initiative by forgiving them in the same way that Christ forgave you. Let them see in your actions the Christ who is eager to forgive every person.

Take the Initiative in Forgiving

The best way to cut the line to resentment is to take the initiative. Forgive the one who has wronged you unjustly, whether that person requests your forgiveness or not. This is why resentment is so much harder to resolve than guilt. We have been taught that we don't have to forgive people's offense against us until they ask our forgiveness and make things right with us. Not to forgive in advance of their request for forgiveness tends to harden their hearts, it keeps the door closed on the relationship and gives us a reason to continue to harbor hate. It's really rationalized hate.

When someone wronged me in the past, my following that formula did nothing to remove my feelings of resentment toward them. In fact, my resentment increased because of their stubborn refusal to *request* my forgiveness. Instead of soothing my conscience, playing the game of "I will forgive you *if* you will ask me to forgive you" only served up more trouble. What about all those scriptures that insist I love and pray for my enemies and return good treatment for wrong? Shall I just ignore them and continue to resent the person who wronged me?

In that situation, I know only one way to deal with the problem of resentment. I must follow the example of Christ who willingly suffered unjust treatment in order to demonstrate his love for abusive people. Peter expressed the thought in these words:

> To this you were called, because Christ suffered for you, leaving you an example, that you should follow

> in his steps. He committed no sin, and no deceit was found in his mouth. When they hurled their insults at him, he did not retaliate; when he suffered, he made no threats. Instead, he entrusted himself to him who judges justly (1 Peter 2:21-23).

Peter's purpose in impressing these thoughts on our minds is to prepare us to accept his exhortation in chapter 3:8-9. "Finally, all of you, live in harmony with one another, be sympathetic, love as brothers, be compassionate and humble. Do not repay evil with evil or insult with insult, but with blessing, because to this you were called so that you may inherit a blessing."

"But it will cause me to suffer!" So what else is new? Christ suffered unjustly to forgive you, and he expects you to pay the same price to forgive others. "Forgive as freely as the Lord has forgiven you" (Colossians 3:13, *Phillips*). "Be as ready to forgive others as God for Christ's sake has forgiven you" (Ephesians 4:32, *Phillips*).

It's tough to forgive because it's so costly. If you've wronged me, it means that I must bear the suffering you've caused me, in order to bless you with my forgiveness. The person who takes the initiative to forgive pays a tremendous price. For instance, suppose someone has slandered you and ruined your reputation. You must be willing to bear the loss of your good reputation in order to "Forgive as freely as the Lord has forgiven you." That's tough. But with God's help, it's possible. After all, look at the reputation Christ gave up for you.

Resentment Is Suicide

Another slogan of Alcoholics Anonymous that should be adopted by every person says, "Resentment is suicide." They say the biggest enemy to the alcoholic is resentment. They know that allowing resentment to linger for long drives you back to the bottle. And the bottle will kill you.

But how do you get rid of the resentment? Just give it away. Dump it. Don't wait until you can trade it for a request of forgiveness. It's like pulling the pin on a hand grenade and releasing the grip. You can't just stand there holding it in your hand. You've got to toss that thing away before it blows up in your own face. Holding onto resentment is suicide!

Perhaps you're thinking: "Faulkner, you don't understand how difficult that is." But I do know a little bit about resentment.

I remember a few years ago my family was out water skiing. The lake was cold, and everybody had skied pretty well the last time around. My buddy said, "Well, Paul, it's your turn."

I said, "Well, it's just about dark; so I'd better go if I'm going to."

So I jumped in the water and climbed into the skis. With no warm up or anything, we started out across the lake. Pretty soon we came to a smooth spot. So I dropped one ski and tried to get my bare foot on the back of the slalom ski. Before I could get my foot into the toehole in the back of the slalom ski to control it, my buddy decided to give me a joy ride and rammed the boat into "go for it" gear.

He turned the corner at high speed, and I was still struggling to get control of the one ski when I started skipping over the tops of the waves. But I wasn't going to give up. I was going to hang on, no matter what! Finally, the only thing I could figure to do was to jam my foot crossways across the back of that ski to control it. Well, see, I didn't realize *my* foot's about a foot *and a half* long, and it stuck out six inches on both sides of that ski. When the water hit my foot, it stripped it off the ski and pulled the hamstring in the back of that leg, sort of like pulling taffy at the fair.

Boy, I was in agony! So I went to the doctor, and he said, "Oh, it's just a lazy muscle. Don't worry about it."

Then I went to a specialist, dragging my leg behind me, and he said, "Oh, it's just a lazy muscle. It'll be all right." So I drug it around for a year or so.

Finally, about a year later I went to a doctor friend of mine and said, "Doc, now I'm not a physician, but I can feel a hole back here in the back of my leg. And it didn't used to be there."

He took a look at my leg and said, "Oh yeah, Paul, you've got half that muscle gone."

So I said, "Well, Doc, just grab that sucker, pull it back up and staple it back where it belongs."

He said, "We could have done that a week, even three weeks after it happened. But the muscle won't stretch back out now. It's all wadded up down there, and it'll never stretch back out. It's too late to fix it."

Talk about resentment! I had a bad case of it against those first two doctors for a good long time. I felt like suing. But God came to my rescue and helped me cut the line of resentment and get on with living.

Triumph Over Resentment

One of my greatest personal triumphs occurred a few months back. I boarded an airplane, and seated there was the specialist who had examined my leg. I could joke with him, and I actually enjoyed visiting with him. I felt no compulsion to talk about the raw deal I earlier felt he had given me. In fact, I felt no resentment toward him at all. I don't know where that resentment went. I do know that it was not of my own doing. God was at work in me, empowering me to love and to forgive him.

Compared to the triumphs others have made over deep feelings of resentment, I regard my personal victory as puny stuff. An acquaintance of mine had a severe, chronic leg pain. A physician told her there was only one thing that could be done to relieve her pain. A nerve would have to be severed in her spine. It would cause the leg to be numb, but she would feel no pain, and the leg could still be useful. She went into the hospital, and they performed the operation. When she came out of the recovery room, she was paralyzed from the waist down. Permanently. Later, her husband left her — a tough combination of resentments was staring her full in the face.

What would you do if you witnessed your four-year-old son's anguish as he died by degrees from lukemia? What do you say when the mother turns toward you and says, "How can a loving God let an innocent little four-year-old die this miserable and painful death?"

Can you resent God? I love the God who permits you to resent him and to express your feelings of bitterness toward him. Remember how he permitted Job to express his feelings of bitterness and resentment? (It's okay to fuss with God, you see. Some *religions* don't permit that, but the Bible does.) Job cried out in his bitterness, "I want an umpire between us," which was his way of saying, "God you've given me a raw deal, and I want someone to settle the dispute between us who will deal with me more fairly." And God deals with Job graciously in his own good time, and he will do the same for you.

That's hard to understand, isn't it? We just don't have a big enough computer to handle these mysteries of life. Some day God will give us a modem hook-up to his computer; then we will be able to compute the mysteries.

Remember the character, Tevia, in the musical *Fiddler on the Roof*? He's mad at God. God has given him five girls, no boy, and now his mule has gone lame. Isn't it great that he feels sufficiently safe in God's presence to fuss with him? If you have any complaints, folks, that's the right place to take them. Your heavenly Father is big enough to take it, and he will help you. Your feelings and emotions are made in his image, too, and he'll understand.

One day I received a letter from a sweet lady who was having a tough battle with feelings of resentment. She wrote:

> It's so hard for me to talk about my deepest feelings. I am limited to a very few people I can be open with about my own struggles. I went in for exploratory surgery at my husband's insistence because of abdominal pain, but I woke up to find that he had given the surgeons permission to do a complete hysterectomy. It made sense to him and to the male doctors to do it while I was there.
>
> I woke up stunned to find out I was a neutered nothing, neither female nor male. I feel less real than a plastic mannequin in the store. I went in feeling young, capable and energetic, and I came out feeling old and useless and bitter.
>
> I feel violated, as if I had been raped. I used to worry about being raped, and I was always cautious. But what would it matter? I'm nothing anymore. I feel as if my very soul has been cut out and violated. Maybe I can overcome my bitterness toward him for failing to protect me. I've even wondered if it would matter if I had an affair. I don't have any worth, or maybe even any soul left.

Most people would say she has a right to be resentful. But who is the resentment hurting most?

Later, I received another letter from the same woman. Among other things she wrote, "I've read it in Acts 8 all my life, but it finally dawned on me — a eunuch — that God loved the eunuch." Through the years she's had a tough time with resentment. But, with God's help, she's through with it.

I received a letter from another woman. She expressed feelings of keen resentment toward her husband who made her life difficult because of his love for booze and other women. She wrote:

> When my husband walked out the door, I was never sure when he would come back. One time it took 11 months. I did housework, babysat, ironed — in fact,

> just about anything that was legal and moral — to keep my family together. I think, to understand the meaning of resentment, you have to water down last night's beans to feed your children while their father sits there nursing a quart of bourbon.

A woman in Florida was raped, shot in the head by her attacker and left for dead. She survived, but she was blind and mutilated. She later appeared on a television talk show. The interviewer remarked, "You must have a lot of resentment and hatred toward the man who did this."

She replied, "No, I gave that man one night of my life, and I'm not going to give him a second more."

Of course, you can cling to your grudge if you want to. But when you do, you use your strength for this day making yourself and the people around you feel miserable and guilty. Or, you can cut the line to what is behind you through the power of forgiveness and use your strength to strain toward what lies ahead.

HOW DO WE OVERCOME?

How do we overcome the problem of resentment? What is the solution? I dare to say you know the biblical answers to that question already. No doubt, these phrases flash back: "Love your enemies." "Do good to those who hate you." "Overcome evil with good." "Do not return evil for evil . . .; but on the contrary, bless." Understanding these scriptures isn't our problem, is it? The thing that trips us up are those tough decisions required to translate these beautiful ideas into our daily behavior.

Be Vulnerable

To cut the line to resentment, you must choose to become vulnerable to hurt. When you respond to hate with love, to resentment with forgiveness and to cursing with blessing, you will expose yourself to cruel and abusive treatment from a few people, but it's worth it! If you never risk, you will never know love.

Learn to accept rejection. It's a fact of life. Professional writers will tell you they receive 15 to 20 rejection slips for every acceptance notice of their work. Artists paint pictures they can never sell. That's rejection, but they keep on painting. Inventors often fail hundreds of times before they come up with an invention that works and is accepted, but they keep inventing. It's the folks in this life who use rejection as a stepping stone to higher ground that succeed.

Life itself is rejecting you! Time is dragging you toward death. It's simply a by-product of life. And someday life will reject you into eternity. If Jesus, the only perfect one, was rejected, you can expect some of the same. Here's what he said: "If the world hates you, know that it has hated me before it hated you. Remember the word that I said to you, 'A servant is not greater than his master.' If they persecuted me, they will persecute you" (John 18:18-20).

Resisting and fighting against those who have wronged you will serve only to increase your resentment. Freedom from resentment comes from choosing an attitude of vulnerability, which says, "I would rather suffer wrong than to do wrong to any person."

Forgive

Next, you must choose to forgive the person who has wronged you. You must cut the line and "forget what lies behind." As we have previously observed, when Paul said, "Forgetting what lies behind," he is not suggesting a literal forgetting of the past but rather the development of a right attitude toward it. It is true that we can never forget the cruel and abusive treatment that we have received from others. But we can forget to *nurture* those feelings of resentment caused by such treatment.

It's similar to looking at an old cut on your body that has become a tough, permanent scar. When the cut was fresh, it festered and was painful. Now that the cut has become a scar, you've forgotten the pain. In fact, you seldom think of it at all. But you can still see the scar. Similarly, it is possible to *forget* the hurt of past resentments. How? By cutting the line with an attitude of love and goodwill toward the people who have abused you.

Become the Transitional Person

"But my father sexually abused me for 19 years! How can I forgive him? It's not right!"

I heard a therapist give this answer: "You've got to become the transitional person." He said, "The way for you to deal with the resentment you have toward your father and to put a stop to incest in your family is for you to absorb all the hurt and pain yourself. Just blot it up. Say to yourself and your family, "I have blotted and soaked up that abusive treatment of the past. It will not be again. I will be the transitional person who stops the incest, right here."

One lady told me this story about her childhood. "I was an abused child, along with my sister and my brothers. We were all abused sexually and spiritually. The truth is, my parents appeared to be very Christlike in church. When people came to visit unexpectedly from church, my mother hid her cigarettes and love magazines under the couch.

"During the week we'd often see my father beating my mother. She would scream and cry and yell. She drank a lot and slept all the time. Many times my father used my sister and me late at night, and my mother never knew.

"One time my sister told a Sunday school teacher what my father was doing. When the church leaders came to our house, my father was so sweet and said, 'Oh, she's just a little girl that tells stories. She's embarrassed because she's developing now, and I guess she just feels uncomfortable with hugs.' My sister was 12 then, and I was 11. My father acted like it was just a big misunderstanding. He told my sister to tell the men she was sorry for lying.

"My mother was in the hospital at the time, and after the men left, my daddy beat my sister with the belt over and over. He knocked her down and kicked her in the stomach. He kicked our dresser drawer in and broke it, and told us never to tell anyone anything or we'd get a lot more than that. When my mom came home, he told her that my sister and I had been fighting over a dress, and we broke the dresser. Then, of course, we were grounded for a week."

Could that lady blot up the sickness and hurt of the past? Yes. Could she become the transitional person for her family? Yes, she did. I wish you could see her sweet spirit today.

Do you hear what the therapist was saying? He was saying exactly what the New Testament has been saying all of these years. Jesus died on the cross and blotted up all the sins of every person so they might be freed from an unbroken chain of spiritual bondage and death. That's why we Christians love a transitional person, whom we have never seen, with a love that is stronger than life or death. "He himself bore our sins in his body on the tree, so that we might die to sins and live for righteousness; by his wounds you have been healed" (1 Peter 2:24).

And Jesus has given you the power to become like him. You are able, through his power, to blot up the misery and disillusionment of your past. You can take them with you to your own mental cross and hang them up there forever on behalf of yourself and your family and friends.

Keep on Blessing Others

"And then what, Faulkner?" you say.

You just go right on loving, acting better than you feel, doing the things that bless other people, forgiving others whether they ask you to or not and doing good to folks, that's what. You do it just like Jesus did.

"Whew, that's tough."

Yep. But Christians are tough people. They're tougher than any other people on earth. They can *do* these difficult things that other people can't handle. Christians blot up what other folks commit suicide over. They're tough. But sometimes toughness is just wisdom in disguise. Part of their toughness is realizing that hanging on to resentment is tougher than giving it up, in the long run. Sure, it's tough to give up resentment sometimes. But with resentment also come bitterness and hate — a double-barreled backfire. So, what looks like toughness in giving up resentment is really wisdom.

Jesus summed it up this way: "Love your enemies, do good to those who hate you, bless those who curse you, pray for those who mistreat you . . . Do to others as you would have them do to you" (Luke 6:27-31).

Easy? Nope. Possible? Yep. "With man this is impossible, but with God *all* things are possible" (Matthew 19:26).

HARD QUESTIONS

People come to me with three questions about resentments they are fostering. And they're not easy questions, either. They're hard as nails. Have you ever asked them?

How Do You Get Even?

When you've been abused and mistreated, how do you get even? You don't. That's it — you don't. There's no such thing as *even* in relationships. You can't get even. Do you give your mate exactly the same amount that you get? Do you give each of your children exactly the same things? No. It's impossible. God didn't even make us all even, did he? Look around at folks. Some are black, some are white, some are tall, some are short, some have lots of hair, some have none. He made us all different — different colors, different faults, different talents. You just can't get even. You're going to lose every time you try. Listen to Paul:

> Do not repay anyone evil for evil. Be careful to do what is right in the eyes of everybody. If it is possible, as far as it depends on you, live at peace with everyone. Do not take revenge, my friends, but leave room for God's wrath, for it is written: "'It is mine to avenge; I will repay,'" says the Lord" (Romans 12:17-19).

Some women say, "I'll just have an affair, too. Then we'll be even." But two wrongs don't make a right. It just gives the husband another mudball to sling. And because the wife has a stronger conscience than the husband, she feels horrible and blames herself for her faults and his, too. You can't get even.

Trying to get even is like trying to win a puking contest with a buzzard. He's a professional! And you simply can't win playing his game.

How Do You Get Rid of the Pain?

Well, unfortunately, you may have to live with some of it for the rest of your life. Remember the paraplegic woman? She didn't get rid of the paralysis. And the woman who was shot in the head—she didn't lose her blindness. Sometimes you just don't get rid of the pain. But, thank God, you can learn to use that pain to bless other people who have experienced similar tragedies.

You're not alone in your pain, you know. There are a lot of people who have been right where you are. A lot of other people have been abused. A lot of people have had misfortunes. Those people need you to minister to them.

Many of our resentments stem from foolish actions. A car accident that paralyzes, a hunting accident that blinds. Other horrible things happen that are just accidental. You can get mad at life, you can get mad at God, you can get mad at the person who was driving. But does that help you? No. The resentment you harbor will kill you!

But you can reframe the pain into a strength. You can use your thorn in the flesh as a source of power or turn your disaster into a dimple.

By laying your hurts and abuses of the past next to the current hurts and abuses of someone else, you can help draw the festering out of their situation and help them move on to healing. They need you and your reframed pain to help them see the picture as it really is.

It's like the university professor who told me recently how he shared the sudden loss of his son with a policeman whose son had killed himself. He said, "It allowed both of us to find some resolution and peace in the problem of a missing son."

So, use your pain. It is a gift from God with which to minister to his other hurting children.

How Do You Get Rid of the Memories?

Try God. Turn them over to him, and permit him to heal them. He will help you to "forget" through forgiveness.

Remember the story of Joseph in Genesis 44-45? In an attitude of hate and resentment, his brothers sold him to a caravan of slave traders headed for Egypt. In Egypt, Joseph was placed on the auction block in a slave market and was purchased to work as a bond servant in the household of Potiphar, an official in Pharaoh's government. Potiphar's wife brought false charges against Joseph and had him thrown into prison where he would languish, long-forgotten. After more mistreatment and lost expectation of release, eventually Joseph was remembered and released from prison. I believe as a result of his gracious attitude, he was soon promoted and elevated to a position of power in Pharaoh's kingdom, second only to the position of the king himself. Had he not looked at his misfortune positively, I think he would never have gained power in Egypt.

Included among Joseph's many duties as Pharaoh's right-hand man was the supervision of the great granaries of Egypt.

Thus, when a period of long famine in Canaan drove Joseph's brothers to Egypt to purchase grain, they found themselves making their request to their own brother whom they had sold into slavery many years earlier. At that moment, Joseph had complete power over his brothers. He had the power to execute them, to imprison them or to let them go free. Would he take revenge on his brothers who had wronged him? No, but they didn't know it. In their traumatic plight, they remembered their ugliest sin as the cause of their dilemma. "We are guilty concerning our brother . . . That's why this distress has come upon us . . . Now the day of reckoning for his blood has come." Their sin against Joseph, committed so many years earlier, was still in their memories, convicting their consciences.

When Joseph finally revealed his identity to his brothers, he reframed the whole event. He told them not to be angry with themselves for the atrocity they had committed against him. Even though they plotted *evil*, God had used it for their *salvation*. He told them to accept that event as a part of God's sovereignty working in their lives, as his means of preserving their lives and the lives of all the members of their tribe.

If anyone had a reason to be resentful toward his brothers, Joseph did. But he became the transitional person who willingly blotted up their wrongdoing to make things right between them again. He took the initiative in offering forgiveness to his brothers even though they had not requested his forgiveness. He handled his resentments, not by getting even with his brothers, but by placing them into God's hand.

What happened to the old painful memories his brothers had inflicted upon him by selling him into slavery? Interestingly, he named his first child Manesseh, meaning "forgetful one." Why? "For God has made me forget all my trouble and all my father's household" (Genesis 41:51).

The brothers still couldn't believe it. They thought that when their father died Joseph would have them killed. They were scared to death! They thought he was just being patient for their father's sake. Joseph had to assure them again that he had really forgiven them. It was over. He had no resentment. God can do that!

Love Lets the Past Die

Joseph had gotten rid of his slop bucket. And so must you. You simply must learn, like Joseph, to reframe life's rejections and abuses into stepping stones to power.

In his book, *Love Within Limits*, Lewis B. Smedes writes this beautiful and inspiring summary:

> Love lets the past die. It moves people to a new beginning without settling the past. Love does not have to clear up all past misunderstandings. The details of the past become irrelevant; only its new beginning matters. Accounts may go unsettled; differences remain unsolved; ledgers stay unbalanced. Conflicts between people's memories of how things happened are not cleared up; the past stays muddled. Only the future matters. Love's power does not make fussy historians. Love prefers to tuck the loose ends of past rights and wrongs in the bosom of forgiveness — and pushes us into a new start.

Anger shuts down an open mind. When you get angry, you're through solving problems.

A person that's praised is the one who is angry for the right reasons, with the right people and also in the right way and at the right time for the right length of time.

— Aristotle

CHAPTER SEVEN

Keep Cool, Even When You're Hot

It was two o'clock in the morning. I was startled awake by the phone ringing next to my head. I sat up, brushing the cobwebs out of my mind, and answered it on the second ring, "Hello."

A frantic female voice on the other end of the line asked, "Is this the preacher at that church over on the south side of town?"

I said, "Yes, who's this?"

She said, without answering my question, "I just want you to know that my husband came home drunk tonight. He threw his bowling ball through the front window, broke up the color T.V. with his trophies and turned over the china cabinet. He's broken up all my crystal! Would you come over?"

Now, folks, I don't fancy myself as a hero who rides a white steed and comes charging in to save the damsel in distress. And domestic anger is dangerous. In fact, it's a killer sometimes. The Police Department loses a lot of good policemen who are killed while trying to intervene in angry domestic squabbles. They tell me it's one of the most dangerous situations they face.

Well, not being Dirty Harry, I took a little safer path and said, "Uh, I will be happy to counsel with you and your husband in the morning at my office, if I can be of some help. I'd suggest you call the police." I did make myself available the next day, but so far as I know they never took advantage of professional help from anyone.

Several months later, but not until they had lost control of themselves again, I received another call from the same woman, again in the wee hours of the morning. She was again drunk when she called and said, "Do you remember me? I'm the one who called you several months ago about my husband tearing the house apart and breaking up the crystal."

"Yes, I remember," I replied.

"Well," she said, "I just want you to know that tonight *I* did it!"

Folks, I don't have to tell you that's not smart. It doesn't make any sense. It's not normal behavior, and it causes all kinds of problems.

Alexander the Great, I'm told, killed his best friend in a fit of rage. What a tragic mistake! His anger destroyed one of his own most precious relationships.

And you know, living in a nuclear age as we are today, I would venture to say that we might be just one rage away from annihilation. If the president of any one of the 25 nations that have nuclear power capability loses control of his anger, we could be faced with a nuclear winter. Uncontrolled anger is dangerous!

GET A HANDLE ON ANGER

Anger Is Tough to Modify

A quick flash of anger can demolish our best controls, even when we know better. It doesn't take Dr. Jekyll's chemistry to release our Mr. Hyde. Let someone puncture our ego, and Mr. Hyde breaks loose from our control, asserting himself in malice or violence.

The first man to discover the explosive power of a quick flash of anger was Cain in the Bible. Moved by envy and jealousy toward his brother, Abel, he exploded into a rage which ended in his brother's murder (Genesis 4:1-7).

The first thing to understand about anger is that by the time you *lose* control you're *out* of control. We have found in research that when a man reaches the point of losing control, he actually no longer has any control. And he just comes completely unwound. That's why it's so important to get a handle on it early.

Anger Is Supercharged

Anger has an incredible effect on your body. It upsets your normal digestion. It keeps your body from assimilating and eliminating properly because it causes the blood vessels to constrict. At the same time, it sends a dangerous supercharge of blood to the heart, brain, lungs and large muscles. It also causes your eyes to dilate. Maybe that's where the phrase came from that says, "I'm so angry I can't see straight!"

Anger Is a Big Stressor

In the family, in the nation, at the workplace — anger causes stress everywhere. Look at these research facts:

A Harvard psychiatrist said that a person "cannot get sick without a stress factor being involved. Buried emotions of anger and fear are the most important stress factors in physical illness." Do you want to keep yourself healthy? Don't get angry!

Dr. Carl Simonton says that the first trait he found to be at the root of cancer is a great tendency to hold in resentment and anger. Isn't that interesting? He says that often they see amazing remission of the disease as the person begins to deal effectively with buried anger.

Dr. Robert Good was asked, "Why did cancer take so many and, yet, not take others of the same environment, such as identical twins?" He said the answer is the presence of emotional stressors, particularly unresolved anger. "The hormones that the body releases under prolonged stress, including the hormone adrenalin, inhibit the body's normal ability to fight and destroy cancer cells."

A Duke University research group found that anger produces two-to-five times the death rate as does high blood pressure and smoking. That's amazing, folks! Just look at what anger can do to you.

Anger Prevents Problem Solving

Anger shuts down an open mind. When you get angry, you're through solving problems; you've moved into another arena completely. The ability to think logically and problem solve is gone. The door has been slammed shut!

Two people can begin to discuss a problem and go along just fine working that problem out until one of them becomes angry. At that point, the other person usually gets angry, too. Then the anger escalates, and they usually lapse into stony silence. But the problem is not resolved. Anger has shut the door to resolution. Later, because the problem was not resolved, it comes up again; and the whole process starts over. It's a vicious circle.

Research by David Mace shows that about 68 percent of problems are never resolved because anger shuts down the problem solving process.

Anger Distorts the Truth

When you become angry, you tend to make great big overblown statements. "You're *always* late!" "You *never* shut the door!" Anger distorts the truth.

When I was a boy, I would get angry with my sister, and I would make some big overstatement. She would respond by saying, "Would you please write that down and sign it?"

And, oh, that would make me so angry. She knew that I had overstated the case, and she let me know it. Then, of course, I had to back down. Did that ever happen to you?

Anger Is Addictive

Our actions form habits — good or bad. If we become angry repeatedly as our way of handling a problem, it can become addictive. Pretty soon anger is the only way we know how to respond to problems. The old adage says, "Practice makes perfect." But that's only true if you are practicing the right thing. Really, practice makes *permanence*. However you practice something is the way you'll perform it permanently. So if you practice handling problems with anger, it will become your permanent habit. But if you begin practicing anger control, that will become your habit.

Just remember, if you give a speech when you're angry, it'll be the best speech you'll ever regret. And to whom do we usually make those angry little speeches? Who do you get mad at? It's the people we're closest to. We get angry with our mates, our children, our friends, our co-workers. You know what, I have never been mad at the Governor of Connecticut. Why? Because I'm never around him. You don't get deep-down angry at folks you don't know or spend time with. It's that simple.

And that's the reason it doesn't help to change mates, change jobs or move to a different city. All you do is move a different person or group of people close to you to endure your uncontrolled anger. The real cure is to work at *handling* your anger, not changing those at whom you vent it. After all, it's not *who* it is; it's their *proximity* to you. It's people who get in your way. It may be the one sleeping with you that gets in your way, or it might be someone driving another car that gets in your way. Those are the ones you attack, no matter *who* they are.

WHAT CAUSES ANGER?

Much unjustifiable anger can be traced to those knee-jerk responses of infant-like emotions. Anger in a baby is quite normal. It's a sign of emotional aliveness. A temper tantrum by a small child can accomplish what milder methods fail to achieve. But an adult with a hot temper who flies off the handle regularly, pushes other people around like a big bulldozer or bangs his head against the wall when he doesn't get his way is not an example of good mental or emotional health. That adult is really still an emotional baby.

Violated Rights

Feelings arising from an unwholesome anger may also be triggered by our beliefs that we are being treated unfairly. You felt you deserved to get a certain promotion, but your boss disagreed. Your rival got a salary increase and gained prestige. You got mud in your face and feelings of rejection. Steamed? Yes! Why? Because you felt you'd been treated unfairly.

Unrealistic Expectations

You may get a bad case of the "angries" if you have unrealistic expectations about people or situations. An employee, for instance, might expect his company to make exceptions to the company policies for him because, after all, his last company did. But that could well be an unrealistic expectation that only serves to increase his feelings of anger and dissatisfaction with what is otherwise a great job. His expectations were too high.

A husband may have been snapping at his wife for several days, and now she's in a bad mood. He knows what he's done. So he reasons, "If I take her out to eat and to the movies, she'll be in a better mood." Well, maybe. But maybe not. His expectations may be too high in expecting her to change gears quite so easily. So when she doesn't turn flips for him, he becomes angry because his expectations were just too high.

Jesus shows us the right way to handle this one. Ten lepers came to him and asked him to heal them. Jesus told them to go to the priest to get a health document certifying that they had been healed of their disease. On their way, all ten lepers were healed. But only one of them came back to say "Thank you" to Jesus. Was Jesus disappointed? Yes! But was he angry? No. Why? Jesus looks at people through eyes of steady realism. He knows people will not always respond the way he would like for them to. Jesus avoided feelings of anger toward people by not expecting more of them than they are able to do. He responded with love, whether they reacted with appreciation or a total lack of it.

Bruce Barton said this about expectations: "If you expect perfection from people, your whole life will be a series of disappointments, grumblings and complaints. If, on the contrary, you pitch your expectations low, taking folks as the inefficient creatures which they are, you are frequently surprised by having them perform better than you had hoped."

I noticed this quote on a plaque in Sam Walton's office recently. It may just be the philosophy behind his great success with the chain of Wal-Mart discount stores: "Don't treat people as they really are, but as if they are what you want them to become."

WAYS TO BLOW IT WITH ANGER

There are three ways to handle anger. The first two ways are the ones we normally use, but the third one is the best. Let's look at all three.

Vent It

Some psychologists recommend that you vent your anger. "Get it out. Blow up. Get it over with. It's bad to hold it in," they say. Well, it is bad to just hold anger inside you. But is it always good to vent? Yes, if you vent *positively*.

"What do you mean, Faulkner?" Well, take your anger out in a positive way. Go out and work in the yard or the garden. Fling dirt, dig up weeds, kill bugs. Put your angry energy to work for you. But *don't* get in the car and go for a drive! That's not a positive way to vent your anger. That's a negative and, possibly, hurtful way to vent your anger.

The Bible says, "Do not make friends with a hot-tempered man, do not associate with one easily angered" (Proverbs 22:24). And again, "A fool gives full vent to his anger, but a wise man keeps himself under control" (Proverbs 29:11). Finally, "A hot-tempered man stirs up dissension, but a patient man calms a quarrel" (Proverbs 15:18).

So you just can't vent negatively. It tears up relationships and friends. It causes illness and all sorts of other problems.

Stuff It

Some folks react to anger in just the opposite way. They suppress it. If someone makes them mad, they clam up. They stuff their anger down inside themselves and do a slow burn. It's like pushing poison into your system. As John Powell said, "When I repress my emotions, my stomach keeps score." And he's right! Stuffing anger can cause stomach aches, nausea, ulcers and other physical health problems. So if you value your health, don't stuff your anger.

"Well, Faulkner," you say, "make up your mind. First you said I can't let my anger out, and now you say I can't hold it in. So what am I supposed to do with it?" Good question.

PREVENT IT

The key is prevention. You might say, when it comes to anger, that an ounce of prevention is worth a pound of apologies. Just don't let yourself get angry. The Bible says it this way in James 1: "Take note of this: Everyone should be quick to listen, slow to speak and slow to become angry, for man's anger does not bring about the righteous life that God desires."

Don't let your anger misfire. That's the bottom line. You have to catch it in the trigger stage. As soon as you squeeze the trigger and the gun goes off, it's too late. You've already shot somebody down with your explosive anger. You've got to stop yourself *before* you pull the trigger. You have to prevent your anger.

There's one scripture I'm glad is in the Bible. Nahum 1:3 says, "The Lord is slow to anger . . ." Boy, am I glad about that! Can you imagine what kind of shape we'd be in if God was trigger-happy? It takes a lot to make God mad, and I'm glad because I'll bet I push him to the limit almost every day of my life. God prevents his anger from misfiring against us.

For instance, can you imagine how angry God must have been with the people who crucified his Son? And, yet, he didn't destroy them. He didn't send down bolts of lightning to turn them to ashes. Instead, he forgave them. He reached down in love and saved them.

How do you know when someone is angry? What are the signs that tip you off that someone is becoming angry?

One thing that happens is a change in their tone of voice. It gets higher, louder or more strained in some way. You cannot get angry—not hot-under-the-collar angry—and maintain a sweet, calm voice tone. It's next to impossible. Your voice is going to come up.

I tell you what else comes up when anger strikes: the staccato inflection of your voice. In order to make your angry point with someone, you begin to emphasize every . . . single . . . word . . . that . . . you . . . say!

Another reaction that tips your hand might be a lapse into total silence. I know why you do that, too. It's an attempt to control your reaction to anger. You think to yourself, "If I say one word, I'll explode." Silence is like a cork in a carbonated drink that's been shaken up real hard. If the cork comes out of that bottle, Coke is going to erupt all over the room. So you keep the cork tightly stuffed in the bottle. But your silence belies your anger almost as loudly as your angry words would.

And then there are those folks who get red-faced when they're angry. They can control their verbal reaction to anger, but they can't control their sensitive skin. You can see a red wave of anger crawl up their neck and into their face. And you know immediately that they are angry.

How should I respond to signs of anger? Respond quickly! As soon as you see one or more of these tell-tale signs of anger, act quickly. To prevent the anger getting out of control, say, "I must have messed up. I must have said the wrong thing. Help me out here. Where did I go wrong?" If you act early on, the person will help you. You can say, "That's not what I meant to say. Let me come at it a different way." But you can't do it five minutes from now because by then nobody is listening to anybody — anger has pulled the trigger, and you're out of control.

Do you ever make someone angry on purpose? I'll bet you know where the "hot buttons" are in people you're close to, don't you? You know just what to say to make your mate or your best friend get on their soapbox. You know the subjects and words that jerk their chains. You know how to "get a rise out of them." Just remember, anytime you do or say things that you *know* will cause another person to become angry, you've done it on purpose, and that's not fair.

There's a good biblical example of this. Paul was called in before the Jewish Sanhedrin council because he'd been accused of trouble-making with his preaching about Christ. And they were giving him the once-over without pulling any punches. But Paul knew where the "hot buttons" were in the council. And he knew how to take their attention off himself and put it onto each other.

The council was made up of Pharisees and Sadducees. The Pharisees believed in the resurrection from the dead, but the Sadducees didn't. And it was a matter of hot contention.

So, Paul simply said, "I stand on trial here because of my hope in the resurrection of the dead" (Acts 23:6). Suddenly, the place broke into a heated, angry debate. Paul had *purposely* pushed their hot buttons, and he got the results he expected.

Now, while Paul was aided by the Holy Spirit to purposely stir up the council's anger, I wouldn't recommend you do it to the folks you know. A real friend will help another *control* his anger, not stir it up. The Bible speaks out against a hot-tempered man, as we saw in the verses from Proverbs, and our job is to help those we love live as God would have them to. Don't push the hot buttons!

Do you ever make yourself angry? Oh, I think we do this a lot! We read things from a negative viewpoint, and then we *choose* to become angry about them. For instance, imagine that you're driving down a two-lane road, and a guy whips around you going too fast and cuts back in front of you too quickly. And you get mad. You immediately assume that he had no good reason for such ridiculous action, and you allow yourself to become angry. Who was it that made you mad? Was it really the guy in the other car? Or did you actually convince yourself to be angry?

Let's look at it another way. Perhaps the other driver didn't see the oncoming car when he pulled out to pass you, and to keep from having an accident pulled back in front of you more quickly than he normally would have. Has that ever happened to you? Or perhaps he had a sick child in the backseat that he was rushing to a hospital, and his mind was not thinking as clearly as it usually did. There might be a dozen reasons why the man did what he did. Why can't we look for the positive side of a difficult situation instead of always concluding the negative? Give folks the benefit of the doubt.

Well, then, how can I prevent my anger from exploding? Delay the explosion. Count to ten. If that doesn't work, count to 100. Or 200! Try to give yourself a few moments of cooling-off time before you respond to your feelings of anger. God says, "Be not hasty in your spirit to be angry . . ." (Ecclesiastes 7:9).

Another way to prevent an outburst of anger is to use your little black book. I used to have a black book where I recorded feelings and reactions that I didn't want to say out loud. I don't need it anymore because I've grown beyond that, but it was a big help.

I remember one day I had gone to play tennis with three other guys. We were going at it full tilt when the courtside phone rang. We stopped the game, and I answered the phone. It was Gladys. She was calling to gently remind me that I had promised to be home by a certain time.

Well, I didn't want to look "wimpy" in front of the other guys. So, I firmly, but politely, told Gladys she was not supposed to interrupt me when I was on the court and that I would be home at such-and-such time. And I hung up. I was steamed.

When I got home, I went straight to the little black book and started to write. I spent the first half page expressing my feelings of anger: ". . . I said I would be home at 6 o'clock, and (I glanced down at my watch. It was 7:15!) . . . ." Whoops. I suddenly realized Gladys had had every right to call me at the tennis court to remind me what time it was getting to be. And I realized what a clod I'd been. So, fellas, I spent the next *four pages* down on both knees in writing asking Gladys to forgive me.

I slinked over to my chair with my tail between my legs and sat down. Gladys quietly walked over and read my four-page entry. She frowned through the first half page, and then began to smile as she read the last four pages. When she finished, she came over and gave me a big old hug, and everything was fine.

But, folks, I want you to know that if I had come into the house and let my anger explode at Gladys, it would have been all over. We'd have had tears — lots of tears — because she just can't take that kind of emotional response. The little black book kept my anger in perspective and *prevented* the damage to our relationship.

The point I'm making is to write it down. If you sometimes blow up in front of the kids, learn to write down your angry feelings instead. One nice thing about writing it down is that it can be erased. But you can't erase angry words once they're spoken.

FOUR STEPS TO PROCESSING ANGER

Suppose you are unable to *prevent* your anger. Then what? Here are four steps to take in order to *process* your anger in a healthy way.

#1 Give Permission to Be Angry

It's okay to be angry. As mentioned before, anger is neither right nor wrong in itself. It's the reaction to the anger that matters. Anger needs to be expressed, but only in a positive way. So give yourself and others *permission* to be angry in a positive way.

Aristotle said, "A person that's praised is the one who is angry for the right reasons, with the right people and also in the right way and at the right time for the right length of time." Whew! There are lots of *rights* in that statement. But I think you can see the need for each one of them.

I know that it's okay to be angry because the Bible says, "In your anger do not sin. Do not let the sun go down while you are still angry" (Ephesians 4:26). It says you're going to get angry. It's a natural response. But you don't have to sin because you're angry. You don't have to let your anger get out of control.

Can anger ever be good? Yes. It can be good when it's directed at something wrong. Policemen, for instance, are often angered when criminals are released from prison and allowed to prey on innocent people again. Children are angered by parents who abuse them. Christians are incensed when minority races are trampled on socially by the majority. And all these people use their anger to fight against the injustices in this life. That's good anger.

Jesus used his own anger against the moneychangers in the temple to cleanse the temple of cheaters and thieves. His righteous anger was directed at a wrong. So he was able to make that wrong thing right (Matthew 21:12-13).

In Mark 3 Jesus was angered by the legalistic attitudes of the Pharisees. He knew that their hearts were wrong because they stubbornly clung to their traditional rules and strict laws about the Sabbath day instead of being happy that a man could regain the use of his arm. "He looked around at them in anger . . . deeply distressed at their stubborn hearts." His anger resulted in his condemning legalism and proclaiming the freedom of Christians.

#2 Report Feelings of Anger

Sometimes another person won't know you're angry if you don't tell him. Anger needs to be calmly reported to the one with whom you're angry. It's best to report it immediately: "John, it really makes me angry when that happens." Talk about it right then, if you can.

But wait! It may not always be possible, or preferable, to report your anger immediately. For instance, if you're out to dinner with friends and someone makes you angry, it might be better to wait until you're alone with that person to report your anger. Don't report your anger to someone in front of other people. Do it in private. Reporting anger in public will only provoke anger, not prevent it as is intended.

Try to set a time limit of 24 hours in which to report your anger. If you can't do it immediately, do it within a 24-hour period to avoid stuffing that anger inside you and building up explosive anger. This principle follows the scripture we mentioned earlier that says, "Don't let the sun go down on your anger."

Here's a guy that's been doing a lot of little prickly things at home that irritate his wife. He puts an unwrapped onion in the refrigerator, thinking he's being helpful, and causes her to have to clean out the entire refrigerator to get rid of the smell. But she doesn't say anything to him about it. He leaves the window open at night for a little fresh air and freezes her to death. But she just gets another blanket and doesn't complain. He brushes his teeth and leaves the toothpaste tube uncapped on the sink. And she just puts the cap back on the tube and puts it away, but doesn't tell him it bothers her. She stuffs those feelings of anger and aggravation down inside, thinking she's keeping the peace.

Then after 17 years, one evening the "helpful" husband puts another onion in the refrigerator unwrapped, and she explodes all over him in a fury of temporary insanity. And he's devastated and says, "One lousy onion, and you go to pieces! I don't get it." Of course, it's not *one* lousy onion. It's 17 *years* of unwrapped onions. But he didn't realize it because she never reported her feelings of anger to him.

Here's the point: If someone irritates you, report it to them early on. "Honey, I really appreciate your helping me in the kitchen, but when you put an unwrapped onion in the refrigerator, the smell of the onion ruins everything in the refrigerator, and I have to clean it out. That really rattles my cage! On a scale of one to ten, it's a 12!" Let the person know how you feel so he can modify his actions or discuss it with you.

If irritants are handled one at a time as they arise, anger can be defused. But when they are allowed to build up, an explosion is inevitable.

#3 Make a No-Hurt Contract

It's okay to be angry. And you should report your feelings of anger as soon as possible. But when you are angry, it's important that no one gets hurt. You should make a contract with your mate or friend that when one of you becomes angry you will not hurt each other. You won't hurt each other verbally or physically. You say to each other, "I'm not going to hurt you with words, and I'm not going to hurt you physically."

Words come first. Very few people are hurt physically that have not first been verbally abused, although a man may use physical abuse because he can't compete with his wife's verbal attacks. She has a better vocabulary and can verbalize her feelings so as to needle him and irritate him. He can't compete verbally, so he responds with male physical strength.

The agreement has to be for a no-hurt contract first with words and then with physical abuse. Both must be covered in the contract. We may become angry, and anger is okay. But we will not hurt each other.

#4 Will You Help Me Work Through My Anger?

You're going to become angry. And you may need help to process the anger so you can get beyond it. Ask the person with whom you're angry, "Will you help me work through my anger? I need you to help me get over it." Only an insensitive clod could resist this plea for help. And this method permits you to report your anger without attaching any blame for the anger. It will work, if you will try it!

TWO BARRIERS TO ANGER CONTROL

There are two significant things that will stand in your way to correctly preventing or processing your anger. Let's look at them:

Ego

The first of these culprits is your ego. In my case it's a little boy that sits on my shoulder and whispers in my ear. And once in a while somebody thumps that little boy and hurts him. Let me illustrate what I mean.

A few years back, Gladys and I were going to Fort Worth to see about her mother. Her mother had lost her husband a year or so before, and Gladys needed to go take care of her. Now, I didn't want to go. I wanted to stay home, play a little tennis, tend my roses and work on some material for my seminars. I just didn't want to go. But I knew I ought to go help Gladys with her mother. So I was driving along playing the silent martyr. I *thought* I was acting better than I felt about going. About halfway there we stopped to have lunch. After we ordered our lunch, Gladys said, "I'm sorry you're angry with me."

I was shocked. I said, "It makes me angry that you *think* I'm angry."

She said, "But you were silent."

And I said, "Yeah, so?"

"Well," she said, "when you're silent, you're usually angry, aren't you?"

And I mumbled, "Well, maybe so." Gotcha!

You see, folks, Gladys had thumped my little boy. And it hurt my ego. To me, being silent was my way of suffering quietly, of being good and not complaining about how I really felt. It was my way of being a martyr. But to Gladys, my silence meant I was angry. My ego got in the way of processing my anger.

Communication

The other culprit that blocks the anger resolution process is poor communication. And many times it goes hand in hand with ego problems. In our case, Gladys thought my silence said, "I'm angry." But I thought it meant, "See what a good boy I am." I had stopped communicating with her, so all she could do was *assume* what I was thinking and feeling. Since I didn't report my feelings, she had nothing to go on but past experience. And past communication experience with me told her that when I get silent I'm angry.

HOW LONG DOES IT TAKE?

A medical doctor and his wife had been coming to me for marriage therapy for about two months. I asked them, "How are things going, now that you're reporting your feelings of anger?"

They replied, in essence, "We're enjoying it because we're making some progress, and it's proving to be helpful. But we're having more arguments than we've ever had before."

I said, "Great! That's wonderful! You've been married 15 years, and you have 15 years' problems that you've been stuffing away. Now you're bringing these old issues to the surface one by one and dealing with them in a non-hurtful way, which you wouldn't dare do earlier. You've learned how to do that so that it's no longer threatening."

Depending upon how long you've been stuffing problems away and not reporting or dealing with them, is how long it may take to resolve all the past issues once you begin. But hang in there! It'll be worth it! Your relationships can be better — much better — than you think, if you deal with the issues in this way. Keep bringing those problems out, one at a time as they arise, and you'll never have more than one issue to handle at once. Life goes along much more smoothly that way. The ripples are smaller in your pond.

CONFLICT RESOLUTION

It's important, now that you've figured out how to report your feelings and take your anger apart to process it, to know how to put things back together. In other words, now that you have seen what makes things go wrong, how can you make them go right again? How do you resolve the conflict?

Be Understanding Before Seeking to Be Understood

You have to seek to be understanding of others before you expect to be understood by them. Work at understanding the other person. Ask questions to find out if you are understanding the other person correctly. You might say, "I heard you say . . . Is that what you meant? Am I understanding you correctly?" Or say, "Let me repeat to you what I heard you saying to make sure I understand what you mean. I'll paraphrase what I think you said. I want to be sure I'm hearing you right."

Give In

Now, you're not going to read this one in many books today. But you will read it in *the* Book. Acquiese. Just give in to the other person. Let the other person have his way. Say, "It's really no big deal to me, and since you obviously have some strong feelings about this, I think we should just go ahead and do it your way."

Oh, how we like to have our own way! Doesn't it hurt just a little bit to give in to someone else? It's almost like being defeated. But there's no contest here. I really believe that one of the most noble and courageous things you can do is to give in to someone else. It's often the most loving thing you can do.

Say a couple is out looking for a new car to buy. She wants a green one. He wants a stick shift. So why not let her have a green one, fella? You don't much care what color it is anyway, as long as it has a great engine and runs well. And, ladies, he wants a stick shift. So, why not? After all, it will save gas, and you already know how to drive it. Give in a little; that's what we're saying. Save your "ace" or "brownie points" for a time when you really, really want something that's important to you.

Win/Win Theory

A third thing you can do is to negotiate a resolution. Try to find an agreeable solution where both people gain something. It's called "win/win"—I win and you win. It's accomplished by old-fashioned horse trading or bartering. "I'll give you this, if you'll give me that."

You need to adopt an attitude that says, "Unless you win, I don't win either." For instance, "Where shall we go on vacation this year?" Well, I want to go to Florida, and you want to go to Colorado. So, we horse trade—this year we'll go to Colorado, and next year we'll go to Florida. We both win! The key is *equity*, not equality—fairness, at least in the long run. It's how we can win together and not a competitive you-win-I-lose.

Agree to Disagree

There are some subjects about which two people can never agree. And that's okay. It is not necessary that two people always agree. For instance, Gladys and I just don't agree about where the thermostat in the hall should be set. We haven't agreed about the thermostat since we got married, and we probably never will. But it's okay because we have simply *agreed to disagree* about that.

Let me tell you how this all came about. Years ago I said, "Honey, just set the thermostat at the temperature where you would like it, then leave it alone." But that didn't work. She just kept moving it up or down anyway. So a few years later I said, "Gladys, let me tell you how a thermostat works. See, there are two kinds of metal within this thermostat that are bonded together. When they begin to get hot, they will warp and make contact in one direction, and when they get cold, they warp and make contact in the other direction. That turns on the heat or the cool to keep the temperature within three or four degrees of where you set it. So, you can set it wherever you want to and leave it alone, and it will keep you real comfortable."

But that didn't work very well either. She still kept moving it up and down. A few years later, I tried two or three other approaches that didn't work. Finally, I thought I'd take another shot at it and said, "Honey, let me tell you how a thermostat works."

She said, "Yes, Paul, I know. There are two little pieces of metal that are bonded together, and they wiggle back and forth to adjust the temperature. But the problem is that they don't know when *I'm* cold and want to be warm. And they don't know when *I'm* hot and want to be cool!"

And I thought, "You know, that's not bad logic. I don't like it, but it's not bad." But there's something in my cognitive male domain that says, "When you set the temperature on the thermostat, you ought to leave it alone. If the experts tell you this is the right temperature setting for maximum efficiency and comfort, then that's where it ought to stay." Needless to say, those experts don't live with Gladys!

See, folks, there are some things in life that are just not important enough to argue about. We just agree to disagree about the thermostat, and Gladys moves it up and down when she wants to. After all, a $20 thermostat is not worth putting stress and tension on a $20 billion marriage. Just agree to disagree and get on with more important matters.

KEEP COOL, EVEN WHEN YOU'RE HOT

Gladys has the answer to keeping cool when you're hot. She simply adjusts the thermostat. And, you know, that's what you have to do. You have to adjust your anger thermostat to keep cool, even when you're hot. It's not quite as easy as moving the little thermostat needle up and down, but it's certainly a lot more important. And it *can* be done!

The key is to learn to vent it positively, not stuff it away, prevent it when you can and process it when you can't. That about sums it up.

By people we are broken, and by people we are put together again.
— John Drakeford

He gave us the ministry of reconciliation . . . and he has committed to us the message of reconciliation.
— (2 Corinthians 5:18-20)

CHAPTER EIGHT

MAKE YOUR RELATIONSHIPS RIGHT

There are no happy hermits. God planned it that way. He created us as social beings who depend on one another. Things just couldn't be right without people. When things go wrong between you and other people, you're in real trouble. And you have to have people to make them right again.

Do you remember the song that said, "People who need people are the luckiest people in the world"? It's a beautiful sentiment. But, actually, people who need people are the *only* kind of people in the world. And when people withdraw from other people, it's a sure sign that life is becoming grim and miserable.

In fact, Dr. Bevers, noted psychiatrist and family therapist, points his finger to "a deficiency of satisfying experiences with meaningful others" as a leading cause of mental illness.

BY PEOPLE WE ARE MADE

One Jewish rabbi said, "Anyone who goes too far alone . . . goes mad." God gave us things to use and people to love. But we often get them reversed and begin loving things and using people.

A student who came to my office for counsel said, "I wish there were just one person in the world to know me and understand me. I feel like one page out of a thousand-page book that's never been read."

That's real loneliness. I'd hate to think that I could live 60 or 70 years and die without anyone ever really knowing me. I don't believe I could even live one year without intimacy with another person. That's one of the things I most appreciate about Gladys. She knows all my idiosyncrasies, my pride and my vanity. And she still loves me.

Have you ever thought to yourself, "If they *really* knew me, they wouldn't love me"? The truth is, if you withhold who you really are, you can never know that you are really loved. You can only be loved to the extent that you are known. Think about that for a minute. Don't you have to get to know someone before you love them? And the better you know them, the more you learn to love them. That's why people get married! The more they know each other, the more they love until they begin to think, "I want to know all there is to know about him."

Isolated Luxury

If I were a billionaire and could promise you anything you wanted, what would you say? Would you say, "Thanks, I'd like a five-cylinder turbo Mercedes"?

And I'd answer, "Yes, of course. Would you like it in red, black, silver, beige or blue? I know, I'll just send you one of each. What else would you like?"

"Well," you say, "I've always wanted a house — a mansion really — with an olympic-sized swimming pool and all the trimmings."

"It's yours. What else?"

"Let's see, would you hang a few Rembrandts on the walls, fill the closets with expensive suits and on and on?"

You say, "Faulkner, what's the catch?" Oh, well, there is one little hook, but it's not a very big one. You'll have to enjoy all these things alone, on a deserted island. You'll be isolated and have no contact with any other person for the rest of your life. Would you do that?

"I'd like to try it for about a week," you say. Yes, but you wouldn't want to stay for the rest of your life, would you? I dare say, most of us wouldn't last a week. Do you know why? The main reason is that we use most of our *things* to impress *people*. "Have you seen my new VCR?" "Have you seen my new T.V? It's stereo!" "Hey, man, look at my new car!" I sometimes wonder which is more important — that I *have* it, or that *you see* it.

Here's the point: if a hermit had $10 billion and everything he desired, he still wouldn't be happy. He needs people to rejoice with him in his good fortune and people to share his things.

WHO ARE PEOPLE?

They are Spirit. They have a physical look, and they weigh a certain amount. But they are spirit. Sure, we will recognize people in heaven, but I doubt it will be by the way they look to us today. We will recognize their spirits. I would recognize my wife's spirit regardless of her physical appearance. Jesus tells us we need to present our spirits perfect to him. I doubt that he cares much about our bodies' appearance, except as the spirit gives joy to the physical appearance. These crumbling old bodies will be changed into vital new bodies, and our spirit is going to return to God from which it came.

THINGS DON'T HONOR US, PEOPLE DO

I remember at breaktime at one of my speaking engagements a guy who came up to me and said, "Dr. Faulkner, on our anniversary I gave my wife a $3,000 ring and a $25 plaque with a little poem inscribed on it I had written to her. Which present do you think she appreciated most?"

I said, "Of course, the plaque."

He couldn't understand how come. In fact, he brought her up at the next break and said, "I want you to see this ring. I spent $3,000 on it." And it was beautiful. But he just didn't realize how much more people are honored by sincere loving words than things—even expensive things.

WHY SHOULD I LOVE PEOPLE?

Good Medicine

People are dirty and deceitful. They will lie to you and cheat you. People will hurt and betray you. They might even kill you.

Do you remember Dian Foosey? She was the girl who turned her back on people to go off and live among the gorillas. She said, "When you learn about the dignity of gorillas, you don't want to be around people."

Recently, some of those people Dian didn't want to be around did come around. For no apparent reason, they killed her. So, it seems Dian had a point. After all, it wasn't the gorillas who killed her, but people. But there is another angle to be considered in viewing this tragic event. When Dian needed protection from her assailants, the gorillas made no effort to defend her. When she lay wounded and dying, no gorillas came to administer medical treatment or to pray for her. They didn't come to hold her hand or to comfort her. What Dian needed most in her final moments was some of those good people she didn't want to be around.

While I was studying integrity-therapy in graduate school, John Drakeford, one of my major professors, used to say, "By people we are broken, and by people we are put together again." When you add to that statement the dimension of God's activity in your behalf, you'll have a pretty good handle on what is necessary to make things right when they go wrong. You've got to have God. You've got to have people. People are good medicine — not only for emotional health, but for physical health, too.

Lisa Berkman and her colleagues at the University of California in Berkeley made an intensive study of 7,000 adults over a period of nine years. They found that people with weak social ties to others had a two-to-five times higher death rate than folks with strong social ties. That's a startling statistic! They're saying that a person with few or no friends is far more likely to die prematurely than a person with a lot of friends. This finding held true, regardless of whether the people smoked, drank, exercised, jogged or were overweight. The bottom line? Loving people is more important to healthy living than good health habits. (Now, just because you love people, don't grab your cigarettes or start "pigging-out" on chocolate fudge sundaes. You can still live longer and better without them.)

In the Langly study conducted at the University of Syracuse, an investigation was made into the health habits of 400 adult citizens of Rockford, Illinois. They found the people who spent time with friends and neighbors were more likely to engage in good health habits than those who spent little time with others. That's interesting. The more friends you have, the more likely you are to follow good health habits and live longer.

So, do yourself a favor. Love people. Help people. Serve people. It's good for what ails you!

I Feel Better About Me

Another reason to love people is so you can feel better about yourself. I belong to a prayer group that meets on Monday at noon. For years now some of my colleagues and I have gotten together to pray and talk about things that are important to us. If one of these guys had a need, and I didn't know about it, I just wouldn't feel good about myself. I feel that they need me, and there's nothing on earth I wouldn't do for them. That's why I try to stay in touch with them — to be aware of their needs and try to figure out how I can help.

But who's the counselor's counselor? In my case it's these same fellows in my prayer group. While I'm looking out for them, they're looking out for me. I trust them explicitly. I'd trust them with my wife, my kids, my money, my problems — anything. I need them. And knowing that they care about me and would do anything for me is a source of great personal fulfillment. And I hope they can say the same about me.

People make you feel better about yourself, don't they? When you feel like you've really messed up a relationship with someone special in your life, what do they often say? "Oh, Paul, that's okay. I make mistakes myself sometimes. Nobody's perfect." Whew! That's a relief. Now I feel better.

How else do people make you feel better about yourself? Well, they pat you on the back when you do a good job. They smile broadly when they see you coming and let you know they're glad to see you. Sometimes, when you've really outdone yourself, they give you a standing ovation. Or, perhaps closer to home for many of us, they give you a promotion or a raise on your job. They listen closely to what you have to say, letting you know they think you're worth hearing. They ask you questions, indicating they think you are a source of valuable information. And on and on it goes.

I just don't know what people do without other people they love and trust. I don't see how they get alone without people who care and are genuinely interested in them. God knew it. That's why he gave us the church as an extended family and source of close friendship . . . a place to belong. When we need support, they become a crutch. When we need encouragement, they become a springboard. They cry with us, laugh with us, celebrate with us and work with us. We are inseparable; we are one. They make me feel better about me.

People Are a Better Investment

Apart from their value in demonstrating love and care for people, things just aren't very important. My mother is 92 years old now. A few months ago I asked her, "Mama, what can I get you for your birthday? What do you really want?"

She said, "Paul, I don't need many things."

What does Mama mean? Mama needs a hug. Mama needs a kiss on the cheek. Mama needs a pat on the back. Mama needs a letter in the mail every week. Mama needs telephone calls and visits. Mama needs me. And that's what everybody needs — not a lot of things, but a lot of *you*.

You know, folks, when you're first born you need lots of hugging, holding, patting, kissing. And when you get old, what do you need? Yep, a lot of hugging, holding, patting, kissing. So why is it that in the middle years between being a baby and getting older you spend so much time trying to acquire *things* when you don't need 'em either *coming* or *going*? What you need is other folks with whom to share life and love and God.

One of our dear friends who has gone with us on a number of tours has become "tourist wise." She has begun buying less and less tourist junk on foreign trips. She says, "I used to think people would be interested in all that junk, but they're not really impressed with my pictures or the junk I buy. Now I shop and buy with *people* in mind. I buy what I think *others* would enjoy having, rather than what will impress them. And that's made all the difference."

Joe DiMaggio told a friend of mine something interesting about the late Marilyn Monroe who committed suicide. He said, "She had everything to live *with* but nothing to life *for*." What a sad epitaph.

And Jesus said it this way: "Do not store up for yourselves treasures on earth, where moth and rust destroy, and where thieves break in and steal. But store up for yourselves treasures in heaven, where moth and rust do not destroy, and where thieves do not break in and steal. For where your treasure is, there your heart will be also" (Matthew 6:19-21). And, folks, laying up treasures in heaven has just got to involve people, not things, because it's people who will go to heaven, not things. You see, people are a much better investment, and the return on your investment will be out of this world!

Jesus invested himself in people. He poured out his blood for people. He loved people. And that's what he wants us to do. "A new command I give you: Love one another. As I have loved you, so you must love one another. By this all men will know that you are my disciples, if you love one another" (John 13:34-35).

People Are Made in the Image of God

Another reason to love people is because they are made in the image of God. So, hooking up with people we can love is like hooking up with God in a lot of ways. Every person in the world is like God and his precious Son. They are God incarnate all around us. They are his Spirit poured into human molds for a time. They are the heart and soul of the Creator of the universe miraculously tucked away into tiny earthen vessels that we can touch and talk to and love. God has given himself to us in the form of people.

Don't you see, that's why we can't treat people with less than the highest dignity and honor. That's why we can't curse and rail at them. That's why we can't use them as some object to be emptied and tossed aside. People are the embodiment of God himself, his most treasured creation, his most precious and special gift to us. And that's why when things go wrong in our relationships, it takes people (God himself) to make them right again.

GETTING RIGHT WITH THE WORLD

People are not getting along very well with one another in Ethiopia, Iraq or Iran. There are dozens of skirmishes going on in the world today because people are making little or no effort to correct relationships that have gone wrong. Can you imagine a professional representative of the United States in Guatemala asking a recently arrived missionary what was going on in *Guatemala*? Well, it happened. The U. S. representative couldn't even speak the native language. He was so ill prepared for his job and unwilling to get out of his office to see what was going on. As pointed out in *The Ugly American*, we Americans don't seem to be very good at loving other nations. And we're not very well liked by most foreign powers because of it.

For instance, Japan is being criticized by the U. S. for not buying more American products to balance the trade payments between the two countries. But the Japanese respond by saying, "We would buy your goods if you took the time and effort to learn our language." Ouch! That hurts because have you noticed how many of the Japanese tourists that come to America speak fluent English?

Friends, the world has become much too small a neighborhood for the kinds of backyard squabbles we see everyday. Our backyard squabbles could turn into nuclear holocaust! Nations need each other to survive. Peoples need to reach out to serve each other as neighbors would do. Evidence of this working has been shown by the concerned response of so many nations reaching out to help Ethiopia through the times of famine and drought. Millions of dollars, tons of grain, airplane loads of medical supplies and thousands of qualified people from nations around the world joined together in an effort to lend a helping hand to the Ethiopians. And it worked! The rains finally came, and they are beginning to get back on their feet. Millions of them were sustained in this life, as meager as it may be, by the food delivered to them by their fellowmen of all races and nations. While the job was not perfectly done, you could almost feel a sense of international unity in it all.

YOU AND ME AGAINST THE WORLD

Relationships. That's what life is all about. I can't make it in this life without you. My life is a series of interactions with people, whether on a personal, professional, social or mental level. I have to have other people, both significant and insignificant to me, just to survive. And when my relationship with others has gone wrong, it upsets my entire world until I can make it right with you again. I can't concentrate on my work. I can't have a good time. I can't eat or sleep right. My world is a mess until I can know that things are right between us. And that's good.

Have you ever seen a couple of lovers who are on the outs with each other? Talk about the world being upside down! She's calling her best friend to talk it over and figure out what to do. He's out buying candy and flowers, making fancy dinner reservations and trying to decide how to apologize. Everything's in a frenzy until they can get things worked out and back on the right track. It's tough working out relationship problems sometimes . . . but it's worth it. And, as you probably know, often the "making up" is the best part of it all.

One plaque that I saw says, "Lord, help me to remember that nothing is going to happen to me today that you and I together can't handle." I like that. Taking on the world is based on a relationship! When my relationship with God is right, there is absolutely nothing that can go wrong that he and I together can't handle.

People. What a delight they are to our lives! What a blessing they are from the Lord. And how precious our relationships with each other should be to us.

CHOSEN PEOPLE

If you're like me, you have special people that you have chosen to share your life. You have chosen your mate, and because of that, you have in a way chosen your children. You choose your special friends with whom to associate. You choose your business associates, the church you want to be a part of and other social groups. Let's face it, folks, we're choosey people. And that's okay.

The Lord was choosey, too. And isn't it wonderful to know that he has chosen you? It's true. As a Christian, you have been specially chosen by God. You are the type person in whom he wants his Spirit to dwell. You are the person he has chosen to carry out his tasks and dreams. You are the person he has chosen, because you are a part of his church, to be his bride and the delight of his love. You have been chosen by God over all other types of people in his world. He has chosen to have a very special relationship with you, and he is concerned that your relationship bc right and good.

Listen to the way Peter puts it in 1 Peter 2:9: "You are a chosen people, a royal priesthood, a holy nation, a people belonging to God, that you may declare the praises of him who called you out of darkness into his wonderful light." What an honor!

And it is through you, his chosen friend, that he hopes to also make his relationship with others right. For he "gavc us the ministry of reconciliation . . . and he has committed to us the message of reconciliation. We are therefore Christ's ambassadors, as though God were making his appeal through us" (2 Corinthians 5:18-20). Reconciliation. That's the process of making a relationship that's gone wrong right again.

That is the message of the Bible. And that is the bottom line message of this book. As Paul pleads in this same passage in 2 Corinthians, "Be reconciled to God" . . . and to each other.

Serve one another in love.
— Galatians 5:13

People are unreasonable, illogical and self-centered. Love them anyway.
— Reader's Digest

CHAPTER NINE

Go First Anyway

Karl Menninger, the founder of the famed psychiatric clinic in Kansas that bears his name, was once asked, "What would you do if you thought you were going crazy?"

He replied, "I'd go out and find someone less fortunate to serve."

Life just seems to make a lot more sense when you're helping someone who has more problems than you do. And it's somehow reassuring to be the one helping another person up, rather than being helped up yourself. For instance, when you pass a man sitting on the sidewalk who has no legs and you put a dollar in his cup and take a pencil, you walk away thinking, "My life's not so bad after all"?

It's your perspective on yourself and on others. You see, good relations come from serving one another. When you serve others, you serve yourself, too. You have to just get out there and serve. It's really not all that bad. In fact, it's fun once you get into it.

SERVE ONE ANOTHER IN LOVE

I believe the Bible is the inspired word of the one true and living God. And I believe that in his infinite wisdom

God gave us his church in which we can love and serve each other. "Therefore, as we have opportunity, let us do good to all people, especially to those who belong to the family of believers" (Galatians 6:10). And in Galatians 5:13 he instructed, "Serve one another in love."

How do we do that? Well, the ways are as many and as varied as there are Christians. And the full answer to that question would fill volumes. But Paul gives us some practical ideas in answer to the question in Romans 12. Look at these challenges to us:

- ☐ "So in Christ we who are many form one body, and each member belongs to all the others" (verse 5).
- ☐ "Be devoted to one another in brotherly love. Honor one another above yourselves" (verse 10).
- ☐ "Bless those who persecute you" (verse 14).
- ☐ "Rejoice with those who rejoice; mourn with those who mourn" (verse 15).
- ☐ "Live in harmony with one another. Do not be proud, but be willing to associate with people of low position. Do not be conceited" (verse 16).
- ☐ "Do not take revenge, my friends . . . If your enemy is hungry, feed him; if he is thirsty, give him something to drink" (verses 19-20).

Wow, what a list! Look how often Paul emphasizes the importance of people in your life. They are important. They are an integral part of your life.

Teaching Others How to Live

I have a good friend named Stanley Shipp. Now Stanley's no ordinary guy. He's the kind they used to write about in *The Reader's Digest* feature called "The Most Unforgettable Character I've Ever Met." He's a died-in-the-wool people lover. He is so completely kind, helpful and transparently sincere that people are drawn to him like a magnet. When you see him in action, turning strangers into friends, helping the helpless and caring for the hurting, you look at him and think, "I wish I were like that, too." It's because Stanley's not afraid to go first.

Stanley travels a lot in his work. One day he boarded an airplane on his way to somewhere else. This time, though, the pilot came on the speaker and said, "I'm sorry, folks, but we're experiencing some mechanical difficulties. We'll be delayed for a while. Could everyone please deplane and wait for a reboarding announcement in the terminal."

So, Stanley and the rest of the passengers went back to the terminal to wait. After a rather long delay, the reboarding announcement was made, and everyone went back aboard. And they waited. And they waited. Eventually, the pilot said, "We apologize for the delay. But we are now having another problem and anticipate another delay of 20 to 30 minutes. We must ask you to deplane again and wait in the terminal until repairs are satisfactory." So, they did.

Finally, the announcement came, "Everything's okay now. If you'll reboard the plane, we'll be on our way." So, they did. By now, though, some of the passengers were fuming and visibly upset by the whole ordeal. One fellow walked down the aisle and complained to the stewardess, "I asked the people at the desk for an aisle seat, but I don't think they gave me one."

The stewardess looked at his ticket and said, "No, that's not an aisle seat; it's a center seat."

"Well, I know I asked for an aisle seat because that's what I always get," he fumed.

Stanley, who was sitting in the adjacent aisle seat, took the initiative. He jumped up and said, "Here, you can have this one."

The fellow said angrily, "No, I don't want *your* seat." Then, in obvious disgust, he took off his coat, wadded it into a ball, opened the door of the overhead luggage compartment, threw his coat in and slammed the door shut. Then he took his place in the middle seat beside Stanley.

Well, Stanley sat there for a minute and then got up. He opened the door to the luggage compartment, shook the wrinkles out of the man's coat, folded it neatly, put it back in the compartment smooth and straight, shut the door and sat back down.

A few minutes later the coat's owner sitting in that middle seat beside Stanley said, "What do you do for a living?"

Stanley paused, then said, "I teach people how to live."

The man nodded his head remorsefully and said, "Start teaching."

And the fellow sitting by the window on that row leaned out and said, "Me, too!"

The go-first servant spirit, exhibited so beautifully by my friend Stanley, is pretty rare in today's society, isn't it? It's so rare, in fact, that when people see it in action they are shocked. They are fascinated by it, and they are drawn to it like a magnet. It is so obviously the right way to live that total strangers will ask you to teach them how to do it. And it is the best way in the world to make things right, when things have gone wrong.

The Silent Shout

A gal named Carolyn was secretary to a director in the consulting division of one of the largest corporations in the world. The headquarters building alone housed some 8,000 employees. And the name of the game was *business* — big business.

Next to Carolyn sat a gal named Terry. And this was, indeed, a seeming mismatch of folks. You see, Carolyn was a minister's wife. And Terry was known as the nightlife party girl of the corporation. Terry barhopped at night and "hung over" her typewriter in the daytime . . . when she actually made it in. Her dress was less than appropriate for a dignified office, she smoked and she swore like a sailor. In fact, she was on the verge of being fired.

Now, Carolyn was a very easy-going, happy and dynamic gal. She was outgoing and had strong secretarial skills. She dressed well and used no profanity. She could work well under pressure and handle more than her share of the load. And she often took the initiative to do just that. When she finished her work, she would ask the other secretaries how she could help them. She answered phones when it wasn't her turn. She went after coffee when nobody else would. She worked overtime without grumbling. When she watered her own plants, she watered the other folks' plants, too. She looked for ways to go first as a servant.

At first, some of the people thought she was just playing up to the boss. But she was so consistent in her attitude and actions, even when the boss wasn't around, it soon was apparent that she was entirely sincere. And, you guessed it, she was promoted twice in the first year she was there.

Carolyn often got teased about her "no frills" language and the clean life that she obviously led. And she good-naturedly joked with her co-workers about their lifestyles and who would eventually rub off on whom. But it began to really take effect on Terry. And she began asking Carolyn probing questions about the way she lived. She didn't understand how Carolyn could be so happy all the time, even under work pressures. And she didn't understand why Carolyn took the initiative to ask for more work. She just wanted to know more about how to really *be* happy, as Carolyn seemed to be, and not just *act* that way at "happy hour" every day.

So one day when the opportunity presented itself, Carolyn offered to teach Terry how to live. And Terry took her up on it immediately. They began studying the Bible together, and Terry's life did a flipflop. She became a totally different person, and everybody at the office noticed. She went out and bought new, more appropriate clothes. She quit smoking (without prompting from Carolyn). She developed a "no frills" language. And she began going to church activities instead of bars. In fact, one evening she went home, gathered up all her liquor bottles and emptied them down the sink. She even began developing the go-first servant spirit at the office. The change was remarkable!

The most interesting thing about it all, though, was the reaction of the people at the office. Instead of going to Terry to ask *her* what had happened to change her, they went to Carolyn to find out what *she* had done. They wanted to know how Carolyn had been able to affect Terry in such a dynamic way. One of the managers said to her, "Carolyn, I don't know exactly what's happened to Terry, but I know *who* happened to her. How did you do it?"

You see, folks, Carolyn didn't really have to say a word. It was her servant spirit, happy lifestyle and go-first attitude that shouted to others: "I know how to live! Ask me, and I'll show you how, too."

CHARITY BY STEALTH

One way to go first is by quietly doing charity for those who need it. Charity by stealth is doing something good for someone else without letting them know who did it. It reminds me of the fellow who paid for the meals of two elderly people in the cafeteria without them knowing it.

And I think of a lady in East Texas who heard about some folks in financial straits. So, she went to the grocery store and bought several sacks of groceries. Then she took her little eight-year-old son and drove over to their house. She didn't want to embarrass the people, so she parked her car around the corner and had her son take the sacks of groceries one at a time, sneaking through the neighbors' yards, and put them on the people's front porch. Then, when all the groceries were lined up, he rang the doorbell and ran like crazy to get out of sight. She and her son waited in the car for several minutes and then drove quietly by to make sure they had found the food. What a marvelous lesson that gal taught her young son about taking the initiative and charity by stealth.

There was this little guy named Billy. And it seemed that everything went wrong for him, especially at school. He just wasn't very good at many things. You know the kind, he was always the last kid chosen for any team. Nobody wanted Billy. He was a born loser, it seemed. The teacher noticed the problem and wondered what she could do to help.

One day the teacher was walking home from school, and Billy pulled up beside her on his bicycle and began to peddle at the same slow, steady pace that the teacher was walking. She noticed that, even at that slow pace, the bike wasn't tipping, wobbling or anything. So, to test it further, the teacher just started walking even slower. Sure enough, Billy just slowed down, too, and his bike stayed steady and upright. No matter how slowly she walked, he stayed right with her. "That's amazing," she thought.

The next day during recess period the teacher said, "Hey, kids, we're going to do something different today. We're going to have a slow bike riding contest." And who, do you suppose won? And who do you suppose "made little Billy's day"? It was the teacher with a charity-by-stealth spirit.

GO FIRST, EVEN WHEN IT'S NOT FAIR

It's not always easy to take the initiative or to do charity by stealth, especially when someone has taken advantage of you or treated you unfairly. But it's still the best idea in the long run.

Watchman Nee tells the story about a Chinese Christian who owned a rice paddy right next to one owned by a communist man. In order to irrigate his rice paddy, the Christian pumped water out of a nearby canal by using one of those leg-operated water pumps that make the user appear to be seated and riding on a bicycle. And every day, after the Christian had pumped enough water to fill his field, the communist would come out and remove some boards that kept the water in the Christian's field and let all the water flow down into his own field. That way, he didn't have to pump water.

Well, this process continued day after day. Finally, the Christian said, "Lord, if this keeps up, I'm going to lose all my rice and maybe even my field. I've got a family to care for. What can I do?"

In answer to his request, the Lord put a thought in his mind. So, the next morning he arose much earlier, in the predawn hours of darkness, and started pumping water into the field of his communist neighbor. Then he replaced the boards and pumped water into his own rice paddy. In a few weeks both fields of rice were doing well, and the communist was converted.

There are two ways to handle a situation like this one. One way is to become angry, chew the guy out and take measures into your own spiteful hands. The other way is to become a servant. You just keep on loving and serving until, finally, you gain a hearing for the gospel of God. As Snoopy of the "Peanuts" cartoon strip says it: "A kiss on the nose turneth away wrath." It's how to take wrong things and make them right.

Oh, I know, it's easy to talk about being a servant or to write about it in a book like this. What's tough is getting out there and working until your legs ache, pumping water into the field of a lousy communist who's doing you wrong. But the joy of it is discovering, when at last you have finished pumping, that you haven't been serving a lousy communist at all but a brother in Christ. And the rice in his field that you watered he will now gladly share with you.

WHAT WILL YOU BE WHEN YOU GROW UP?

When you were a little kid, do you remember people asking you, "What do you want to be when you grow up?" And in your wild imaginings as a child, did you ever answer, "I want to be a servant"? No. We went for the important stuff, didn't we? We wanted to be doctors, lawyers, policemen, firemen or supermen. But a servant? No way. And, yet, all these are servants. Some are even called "public servants." Many businesses even advertise their *service* as their most important asset.

Have you ever wondered what the boy Jesus said when his parents' friends said, "Jesus, what do you want to be when you grow up?" Somehow, I just don't think he said, "I want to be a carpenter like my dad." In fact, by age 12 we know he already understood his role. When his parents found him in the temple talking with the religious leaders of his day, he said, "I have to be about my father's business" (Luke 2:49, *KJV*). And he understood that the business was that of being a servant.

As he grew older, Jesus went into full-time *service* in his father's business. His was a glorious service, and yet, there was nothing glorious about washing dirty feet, touching leprous people, smelling the stench of a dead Lazarus or being nailed to a splintered wooden cross that was then dropped in a hole. There were no accolades or kudos for Jesus' lowly servant spirit—only persecution and death. And still he served. He still took the initiative to do good.

One day the disciples of John the baptist came to Jesus. They wanted to know if he really was the promised Messiah so they could go back and tell John who was languishing in prison. Jesus said to them, "Go and tell John what you hear and see: the blind receive sight, the lame walk, those who have leprosy are cured, the deaf hear, the dead are raised, and the good news is preached to the poor" (Matthew 11:4-5). In other words, go tell John you have seen a great servant who ministers to the needy. When you tell him that, because he is such a servant, he will know that I am really the Messiah.

SEEING THE POTENTIAL

Jesus had the miraculous gift of being able to see potential in people that the average person could not see. And it often caused a stir among his disciples. Take the Samaritan woman who came to draw water at the well where he was resting (John 4). Now, most Jews would not have even glanced in the direction of a Samaritan "dog," much less struck up a conversation with a Samaritan *woman*. To them there was nothing lower on the earth. Nobody could see anything potentially good in a woman who had been married, divorced, married, divorced, married, divorced, married, divorced and who was now "shacking up" with some guy who wasn't even her husband. But Jesus could.

So he told her about the eternally refreshing water of life and helped her make all the things right in her life that had gone wrong through the years. About that time the disciples came back from their shopping trip to town. And they couldn't believe it! Jesus, the king of the Jews, was actually talking to a Samaritan . . . and a woman! And the Bible says something very interesting at that point: "But no one asked, '. . . Why are you talking with her?'" They had, evidently, learned that Jesus had insight they did not have into people, and they did not challenge his judgment.

As usual, Jesus was right. This woman had enormous potential for God. She ran back to town. In fact, she was so excited she forgot to take her water jar with her. And before long she had convinced the whole town to come out and learn from this Jesus, the giver of eternal living water. This Samaritan reject evangelized an entire city all by herself! That's what you call potential, folks.

Now, the point I'm trying to make here is that only God can see all the potential in people for his church. You'll note in this story that, if it had been left up to the disciples, this woman would have simply drawn her water and gone back to town unnoticed and unsaved. But Jesus didn't see her the same way. He made the first move. He took the initiative. And that's our job as Christians. Like the disciples, we can't always see the real potential for the Lord in the people around us. But it's our job to go first. We need to tell them about the eternal living water. God may have led them to us because *he* can see their potential, whether we can or not.

It reminds me of a preacher who was conducting an old-fashioned tent meeting many years ago. The meeting lasted two weeks, and during the whole two weeks only one little teenage girl responded to the message of Christ. And the preacher said, "I thought the meeting really hadn't accomplished much." But God had seen the potential of that young girl for his kingdom. A few years later that gal got married. Over time she had seven children — five boys and two girls. And she trained them in the way of the Lord. As they grew up, all five boys became preachers, and the two girls married preachers. And the number of souls that have been saved through that family of preachers is untold! It numbers into the thousands. And all because the church and the preacher took the initiative to teach God's word so others could hear it and be touched by it.

You see, we humans are nearsighted. We see things right up close to us pretty well. And sometimes that's even blurred. But God is farsighted. He can see a person's potential way down the road yonder. So he sends them right up close to us so we don't miss them in our nearsightedness. He sends them right out to the well where we're resting. And sometimes they have to set their water jars right down on our feet to get our attention. That's when we need to get out our go-first dippers and start talking about the water.

WHAT SERVANTS DON'T DO

Servant spirits are such gentle souls. They are pure in motive and humble in heart. Just as a matter of contrast, let's look at some things first that servants *don't* do.

They Don't Care Who Gets the Credit

True servants really don't care if anybody knows what they've done for someone else. They don't get their feelings hurt if the church bulletin doesn't have a special note of thanks to them for cleaning up the teachers' supply room or mopping the nursery. They go quietly about their ministry of service and would just as soon nobody made a big deal out of it. They don't care if they get the credit or not. In fact, they believe the thanks and credit go to the Lord.

They Don't Keep Score

Have you ever been around anybody who's a scorekeeper? "Look what I did for you. When are you going to pay me back?" These are folks who invite you to dinner . . . once. Then, they wait for you to reciprocate. If you don't, they don't invite you again either. Servants just don't think like that.

They Don't Play the Martyr

"Boy, I went over to the benevolent center yesterday and spent five hours down there sorting clothes and stocking grocery shelves. I think I threw my back out, too. It was so hot down there. And you know what, I was the only one there." Poor me. Look what I've done. Servants don't feel sorry for themselves or do their work because it's their *duty*. Rather, they whistle while they work and never complain. Their joy comes from their service.

WHAT DO SERVANTS DO?

Now that we've seen a few of the things servants *don't* do, what *do* they do?

Listen Louder

Some people listen *louder* than others. I like that way of saying it. It may not be proper grammar, but it makes the point that attentive and sensitive listening is hard work. It takes concentrated energy and control. The ears of servants are fine-tuned to sense the vibrations of need in the tones and emotions of the speaker. They pay close attention and look for opportunities to draw you out and help you express what's on your heart.

That's one of the differences between men and women. Women are wired for 440 volts! They have little emotional wires sticking out from them in all directions. They are wired for sound and two-way communication. They talk and receive. They hook into another person's line and listen loudly to that person's emotions and needs.

We men are wired for 12 volts. That's all. We have two little wires sticking out, and they're both bent. Our speakers are usually hooked up, but our receivers are dead. So, we have to work a lot harder to listen loud than the women do. We're just wired up differently. We men are like two tin cans and a waxed string. But the women are hooked up like Ma Bell.

One of my college classmates was a real beauty. She won everything there was to win. Shc just had something about her that attracted you to her instantly. And everybody loved her. I began watching her in a faculty meeting one day. And she just radiated. Her personality blossomed through a very attractive person. And I watched to see if I could figure out why.

It didn't take long. Wc were all sitting in chairs that swiveled. Every time a different person began to speak, this lady would turn her chair to face him. And she just drank him in, every word he said, with her eyes and attention. When the person next to me began talking, she turned her chair and faced me almost squarely on, and that's when I saw it so clearly. She just seemed to breathe in that man's personality. She totally absorbed everything he said, and he knew it. I was amazed and thought, "That's it!" Any speaker picks out those people in his audience. You are drawn to them. You catch yourself looking at them over and over again because they seem to be just sponging up your every word. It's flattering!

Servants are good listeners. They are listening for opportunities. They are listening for hurts to heal and joys to share. Learn to be a loud listener, and you'll be amazed at what will happen to you.

Transparent

What you see is what you get with real servants. They are transparent people. They wear no masks to disguise their real selves from the selves they want to portray. They're *real* people. Now, that doesn't mean they go around "spilling their guts" to everyone who comes along. We don't need that. That's generally just a play for sympathy. But these transparent servants are willing to go first when necessary and share with you some of the hurts and problems they have faced and overcome, in order to help you through a difficult time. They have an attitude that says, "I understand your need and your problem because I've been there, too. Can we talk about it? Can we pray about it together? How can I help?"

The Bible says, "Confess your sins to each other and pray for each other so that you may be healed" (James 5:16). A true servant of God will do that. He will take off his mask and show his real face of love to someone who needs him to. He will become transparent.

Sensitive

Folks with a servant spirit care, really care, about other people. They are gentle and sensitive to the unique needs of others, without regard to their own struggles. I received a letter from a woman who is obviously in love with her husband in a head-over-heels fashion. And after reading this letter, I think you'll understand why. This is a beautiful modern-day version of the Song of Solomon.

> Dear Paul: Jim was 21 when we married, and I was 18. In lovemaking Jim was way ahead of Masters

> and Johnson. He would quote passages from the Song of Solomon as he began kissing the back of my neck and leading me into the bedroom. His favorite passage was about the turtledoves, twins in a row. I loved it.
>
> He made me feel like I was the most beautiful woman in the world. When I was 19, I had a baby and breastfed him. I got mastitis. That year 17 babies died from staph infections, and a few mothers died from mastitis. Penicillin was ineffective in treating my condition, as were antibiotics. I was dying. The doctors tried everything. They operated on me four times. They cut huge gashes in my breasts to allow the infection to drain. After nearly three months of hanging on, a new drug was given to me, and it worked.
>
> When I was able to be home again and to care for our baby, I went into a mild depression. Now I know that it was normal. Then I didn't. I tried to hide it from Jim, but I couldn't. I cried and cried. Jim held me, and I blubbered, "You don't have turtle-doves, twins in a row, anymore." He held me in his arms and gently rocked me back and forth. He kissed me until I stopped crying. He told me that every scar was precious to him and that it didn't matter that my breasts weren't the same size any-more. To him, the scars were symbols. They meant that I was alive and that meant more to him than any other possession. He still kisses those scars and tells me he loves me. He still makes me feel like I'm the most beautiful woman in the world, and once in a while he still quotes from the Song of Solomon.

That's what we're talking about, folks. We're talking about people who can get out of themselves long enough to bless somebody else's life. We're talking about people who are humble.

Look Down the Ladder

You know, we have a stepladder society. Have you ever noticed? We're always wishing we were just one more step up the ladder, and we're usually feeling sorry for those poor folks that are on the rungs lower down than we are. And pretty often, someone steps in our face as they clamor their way past us up the ladder, or we step in somebody else's face doing the same thing. It's a stepladder mentality.

Sometimes we meet someone and come away thinking, "Now, he's my kind of folks. I'm going to make an effort to get better acquainted with him." And usually, when we say "my kind of folks," we actually mean that they look like us, act like us, talk like us, dress like us and occupy the same social rung on the ladder as we do. And aren't most of the people we love and serve those friends we regard as "our kinds of folks"?

We a tend to show great honor to the people "above us" on the social ladder, while loving and serving our social peers, and isolating ourselves from the people at the bottom of the ladder. But servants bend their egos down in love and take the hand of the person on the rung below them in friendship. They also reach up with a servant's hand to the rung above them and offer the friendship of Christ. They are multi-level people, unhindered by a stepladder mentality.

There are probably lots of folks who would like to be friends and fellow servants with you on all levels of the ladder. Some of those on higher social rungs look at you wistfully when they see your contentment with life and happy servant spirit. And those on lower rungs need your care and comfort in difficult times. You just have to broaden your vision from a side-to-side view to an up-and-down view. And if you will look down to the very bottom of the ladder, you'll see Jesus there preaching the good news to the poor, washing dirty feet, healing the hurting and comforting the broken-hearted. He'll be there laying down his life on a cross for crooks and liars and prostitutes. And he'll be motioning for you to come down off your rung of the ladder to join him. "For a servant is not above his master" (Matthew 10:24).

GO FIRST, EVEN WHEN IT'S NOT YOUR TURN

To make things right when things go wrong, you have to go first sometimes when it's somebody else's turn. You have to take the initiative, even when the other person ought to. You may have to say, "I'm sorry. Please forgive me." Yes, even if the other person hurt you. You just have to grab that bull by the horns and wrestle it to the ground.

"But, Faulkner," you say, "that's not fair." You're absolutely right. Do it anyway. Some things in this life are not fair, but they are necessary for survival—either physically or emotionally. You must avoid, at all cost, the stand-off attitude that says, "Well, I will if you will. But I won't if you won't." Don't wait for the other person to come to you. You go first. If you wait *your turn*, it may never come, and the relationship will never be made right. Relationships are too precious to leave to chance. They're the only things that matter in this life.

When the Roman soldiers nailed Jesus to the cross and stuck a spear in his side, he didn't wait for them to make the first move toward making things right. He said, "Father, forgive them, for they do not know what they are doing" (Luke 23:34). He went first, and it was definitely not his turn!

And when no servant was present to wash feet, Jesus didn't wait for one of the disciples who *should* have volunteered to do so. He went first in order to exhibit the true servant go-first attitude to them. According to the example of Jesus, the ladder that leads upward to true greatness is the same ladder that leads down to lowly service. "Whoever wants to become greatest among you must be your servant" (Matthew 20:26).

SOCIAL CONTRACTS

One good way to make things right *before* things go really wrong is to negotiate a social contract with the other person. Now, this isn't some new-fangled legalese document. It's something we've been doing for centuries; we just haven't called it by a name. Here's what I mean.

We all make mini-contracts with each other—spoken or unspoken. If you're married, don't you usually sleep on one specific side of the bed and your mate the other? See, you've agreed to a mini-contract about which sides of the bed you will sleep on. No big deal, but important to peace and harmony.

Recently, Gladys and I went to Wichita Falls to teach an extension course. It was cold when we came into our motel room, so I punched the "Heat" button, and we went to bed. In a few minutes Gladys said, "Paul, when the heat is on, by morning my nose gets dry, and it makes it tough for me to breathe."

I said, "No sweat." And I got up, punched the "Off" button and went back to bed.

Her first words the next morning were, "Paul, did you get cold during the night?"

Through chattering teeth I replied, "Nnnnnno."

She said, "I'll tell you what. I'll make a contract with you. Anytime you turn off the heat so I can sleep better at night and then you get cold, if you'll nudge me awake, I'll get up and turn it back on. Deal?"

And I said, "Deal." So, the bargain was struck, and we've lived according to the terms of that little contract ever since. It was a simple way to prevent an issue from becoming a problem in our marriage.

The key to mini social contracts is to negotiate the issue and make an agreement *before* the issue becomes a problem and a source of trouble. It says, "We know we have a difference of opinion on this point. So, let's come to some mutually agreeable plane where we can both be happy." It works, folks! Give it a try yourself.

ANYWAY

Sometimes you just have to go first anyway, even though it's not your turn and it seems unfair. Just bite the bullet and do it. The end result will be worth it when a relationship that's gone wrong is made right again. There are lots of *anyways* to deal with in life, as this poem, compliments of *The Reader's Digest*, expresses:

> People are unreasonable, illogical and self-centered. Love them anyway.
>
> If you do good, people will accuse you of selfish ulterior motives. Do good anyway.
>
> If you're successful, you'll win false friends and true enemies. Succeed anyway.
>
> Honesty and frankness make you vulnerable. Be honest and frank anyway.
>
> The good you do today will be forgotten tomorrow. Do good anyway.
>
> The biggest people with the biggest ideas can be shot down by the smallest people with the smallest minds. Think big anyway.
>
> People favor underdogs, but follow only topdogs. Fight for some underdogs anyway.
>
> What you spend years building may be destroyed overnight. Build anyway.
>
> Give the world the best you've got, and you'll get kicked in the teeth. Give the world the best you've got anyway.

Choose to die young, no matter how old you are.

In all these things we are more than conquerors through him who loved us.

— Romans 8:37

CHAPTER TEN

Live Young, Even When You're Old

To make things right when things go wrong, make up your mind to die young, no matter how old you are. Whether you are 23 or 83, choose to be youthfully alive as long as you live.

Douglas MacArthur had an essay about age on his office wall. It read: "Youth is not a time of life, it is a state of mind. You are as young as your faith, as old as your doubts, as young as your self-confidence, as old as your fear, as young as your hope, as old as your despair."

One old gentleman said, "The lines on my face are the service stripes of yesterday, which have equipped me to do a better job of helping people today." That's the spirit that keeps him young.

That's quite different from the fellow who wrote:

> I get up each morning, dust off my wits,
> Pick up the paper and read the obits.
> If my name is missing, I know I'm not dead,
> So I eat a good breakfast and go back to bed.

One fella was lamenting the problems of getting old and made up a list called "How to Know When You're Growing

Older." It's light-hearted and true at the same time. He says you can tell you're growing older when: everything hurts, and what doesn't hurt, doesn't work. Your little black book contains only names ending in "M.D." Your children begin to look middle-aged. You look forward to a dull evening. You sit in a rocking chair and can't get it going. Your knees buckle, and your belt won't. Your pacemaker makes the garage door go up when you watch a pretty girl go by. You sink your teeth into a steak, and they stay there. And the little grey-haired lady you help across the street is your wife.

NEVER STOP

Sure, there are some physical limitations imposed by age. But that doesn't have to mean the end of personal growth or the accomplishment of vital plans and purposes. It's not the number of candles on your birthday cake that matters. It's your mental attitude. Never stop dreaming! Never stop believing! Never stop expecting! Keep moving and climbing into your future as long as God in his grace gives you a future. Determine to die young, no matter how old you are.

Jesus died at the young age of 33. And Moses died young at the age of 120, his eyesight undimmed and his natural vitality undiminished. Caleb was still going strong and making one of the most significant accomplishments of his life at the age of 85.

Do you remember Caleb? Forty-five years earlier he, along with 11 other men, had been sent into Canaan to spy out the land which God had promised them. What they discovered was frightening, even though they were young and strong. They saw giants in the land and well-fortified cities. Ten of those soldiers agreed that there was no chance of military victory, despite God's promise. Caleb and Joshua were the only two spies who believed that God would give them the victory. But they were voted down, and for the next 40 years that nation wandered in the wilderness.

Finally, when Israel did enter Canaan under Joshua's leadership, and the land was being distributed to the various tribes, Caleb asked for the most difficult task of all. He said, "Now then, just as the Lord promised, he has kept me alive for 45 years since the time he spoke to Moses, while Israel moved about in the desert. So here I am today, 85 years old! I am still as strong today as the day Moses sent me out; I'm just as vigorous now as I was then, and I can go to battle. Now give me this hill country that the Lord promised me that day. You yourself heard then that the Anakites were there and their cities were large and fortified. But, the Lord help me, I will drive them out just as he said" (Joshua 14:10-12).

What a fantastic spirit. Caleb was 85 years old. Yet, with God's help, he was determined to drive out the giants who lived in large, fortressed cities in the hill country—the most difficult type of terrain to conquer militarily. What motivated Caleb to request this risky task? If anyone had earned the right to retire and live the rest of his life in security and comfort, it was Caleb. But he believed God still had something important for him to do. And he believed, with God's help, he could do it.

PLAY IT AGAIN, VLADIMIR

You may be forced to retire from your job when you're 65 or 70. A lot of businesses and organizations will even pay you more money to retire early. In fact, about the only thing you can do in the United States past age 65 is to become president of it. For a man well over retirement age, Ronald Reagan wears the most demanding job in the world rather well, I think.

But, thankfully, there is no mandatory retirement age with God. He doesn't have any artificial system which tries to force people out at a time when they have so much to offer. All your life up to this point has been preparation for now. So don't quit now or stop growing too soon. You have too much to offer.

Many, like Caleb, have achieved their greatest accomplishments in their autumn years. Pablo Casals continued giving concerts into his nineties. He practiced his cello every day. Someone asked him why, and he said, "Because I think I'm making progress."

In 1925 Vladimir Horowitz fled his native Russia under the pretext of taking piano lessons abroad. And as late as 1980 he claimed, "I have no desire to return. I don't like the Russian approach to music, to art, to anything. I lost all my family there. I never want to go back, and I never will." And, yet, in the spring of 1986 Horowitz did go back to Russia.

Horowitz had announced his retirement at least twice, but at age 81 he gave what may have been his most memorable concert in his homeland. And the response of the Russian people was unanimous: "It's like listening to a legend." And international television recorded that the people "literally wept at his music."

Yes, Horowitz is a legend in his own time. But why? Because he quit while he was ahead? No! Because he keeps playing.

Grandma Moses *started* painting when she was 80. Noah Webster was 70 when he produced his dictionary. Winston Churchill did not reach the peak of leadership until he was well past the age of 65. And Colonel Sanders was a "retired," white-haired old man before he began his Kentucky Fried Chicken conglomerate.

One that gets a little closer to home with me is Gladys. She's not about to give it up. She is determined to learn to wear contact lens, if it kills her. One lens is for distance, and the other one is for close-up. Her middle-aged brain is busy trying to figure out which eye to process, but she'll win — she's a scrapper!

You don't have to be famous to accomplish God's plan for you. Dr. Paul Southern is 80 plus — still growing and going strong. He's the man who hired me to teach at the university when my teaching credentials were not all that strong and despite the objections of some who warned: "He can't do the job."

Well, Paul retired from his job at age 68, but he didn't stop teaching. He went to a northern college and taught there. Then he taught for a while in New Zealand and Australia. Today, this Caleb-like man is teaching four classes at a college in Michigan. At 80 plus, he is still growing and fulfilling God's plans and purposes for his life. He's determined to die young, no matter how old he becomes.

GROWING AND CHANGING

Winners in life are always learning. They are curious — poking around to see how to build a better mousetrap and, thus, a better world. Losers just do their job. They're not curious. They don't learn so they don't get promoted. They're not much fun to be around. They add little to the pool of knowledge in a conversation. And they're the first to complain about change because they have to learn something new. And, as a result, nobody beats a path to their door.

Where there is life, there is growth, change and movement. When anything on God's earth stops growing, changing and moving, it is dying. It's on its way out. There is nothing static about our lives. Nothing. Our bodies are changing. You don't look the same today as you once did. If you don't believe it, look at a photograph of yourself ten years ago. Each moment that we live old tissues and cells of our bodies are dying, and new ones are growing to take their place. A scientist said, "If you want to speak to me, you'd better hurry because I'm changing every minute." And so are we all.

Our minds are changing. We smile today at some of the things we believed yesterday. Our values are changing. Things that were important and significant to us at age 10 seem childish and insignificant to us at age 50. Our characters and personalities are changing because we are changing.

Our friendships are changing. Some of them have become stronger through the years, but others have faded. Our relationships are changing. Knowledge is even changing. Physics, math, business — could a university maintain its accreditation and status if it used textbooks even five or ten years old? Look how much we've learned recently about astronomy from the space shots and Halley's Comet. Our textbooks already need updating again.

The point is: you have to get on the bandwagon! You either have to get in step with the marching, or the parade will simply pass you by. And you'll be left standing on the curb with confetti in your hair and cotton candy on your face wondering where life went. No! Lick off the cotton candy, shake off the confetti and get in step with the beat of life.

DOIN' WHAT COMES NATURALLY

If you want to grow, change and move in the direction of love, there is only one person in a relationship whom you can reasonably expect to change. You know who that is, don't you? The only person I can change is me. Thus, if my relationships are to change, *I* must be the one to initiate the change.

There's a myth going around called Naturalism. The myth assumes that "doing what comes naturally" is the authentic thing. It's the real stuff. And if you have to change or make adjustments, then it isn't natural or real. Hogwash! Many marriages suffer from this myth. In their book *Vitalizing Intimacy in Marriage*, Pat and Robert Travis say, "Many couples feel guilty when they find they have to *work* on their relationships. It is as if they perceive working on their marriage as meaning that they are not successful or that they do not 'naturally' love each other."

This myth grows out of statements like, "And they lived happily ever after," as if you naturally find a one-and-only and all else just flows beautifully like a stream to the sea. Ridiculous. Pardon my grammar, folks, but there ain't nothin' that simple in this life. Most all good things in life require hard work to accomplish. You have to do your home*work* to learn math and English. You have to work hard to learn how to ride a bike, swim or play tennis. The "good life" requires growing, learning, *un*learning and *re*learning. Life is a colon, not a period. There's more to come.

THE GROWTH CONCEPT

The book lying open in front of me as I write this is the miracle book of the world. It's as old as human history and as young as its most recent birth as a new translation. Unlike other books, the Bible is a living, active and powerful message from our Creator which causes growth, change and movement in the hearts and lives of all who hear it and heed it. It is ageless, like its author, and its readers can also remain ageless through its power.

The Bible is filled with growth concepts. One that interests me is what scholars call the "silent years" in the record of Jesus' life. He lived to be 33, but there is no record of his years from 12 to 30. But Luke's gospel has a magnificent summary of those 18 years: "And Jesus grew in wisdom and stature and in favor with God and men" (Luke 2:52). Those were the patient days, weeks and years of study and preparation for the three most significant years ever lived. Even in what appeared to be unfruitful days, our Lord was growing and moving toward the fulfillment of God's purposes and plans for his life.

Jesus says to his disciples, "This is to my Father's glory, that you bear much fruit, showing yourselves to be my disciples" (John 15:8). If you want a bushel of grapes tomorrow, you can't have them by planting a grape seed in the ground today. That tiny grape seed must go through all sorts of growing processes to produce a bushel of fruit. Jesus wants you to bear much fruit by devoting yourself to your own personal growth and development as a Christian. It's a growth concept, you see.

Here's another one: "Make every effort to add to your faith goodness; and to goodness, knowledge; and to knowledge, self-control; and to self-control, perseverance; and to perseverance, godliness; and to godliness, brotherly kindness; and to brotherly kindness, love. For if you possess these qualities in increasing measure, they will keep you from being ineffective and unproductive in your knowledge of the Lord Jesus Christ" (2 Peter 1:5-8). If you want to grow up in Christ and be an effective and productive Christian, Peter says you've got to keep adding to what you've already got. You've got faith? Great! Now add goodness to that. And when you've got goodness, go after knowledge. Don't quit 'til you've got them all.

Physical Growth

Physically we grow slowly and imperceptably until we are about 25 years old. That's when our physical vitality usually reaches its peak. But we are able to retain our physical powers much longer than once thought. According to the Coopers of aerobics fame, the strength of a person at age 60 has diminished only slightly from the plateau he reached at age 25. After 60, physical vigor declines significantly. Yet, amazing physical feats have been accomplished by people in their seventies and eighties.

Jack Lalanne, the well-known T.V. exercise coach, celebrated his seventieth birthday this year by towing 70 boats containing 70 people for a mile across Long Beach Harbor. Amazing! But wait. He did it by holding the rope in his teeth. He was handcuffed and wearing leg shackles!

And think about Noah who was 400 years old when he *started* building the ark. Remember that the boards had to be hewn by hand from gopher wood trees (we'd call them cypress). But you may be thinking, "Sure, Faulkner, but God was giving him the strength to do that." That's right. And he'll give you the strength you need to do the things he has planned for you to do, too.

And will George Burns ever die? He's still making movies in his nineties. He's the youngest oldster I know of. He will definitely die young.

Mental Growth

Research reveals that you can keep on growing mentally almost indefinitely. Oh, we may find it a little tricky to remember numbers and facts as we get older, but the raw level of our intelligence declines only slightly.

There's one old fella I think of named Tillit S. Teddlie. He's 101 years old. He has been preaching and writing hymns since he was 15. Now, in his old age, he is almost blind and doesn't hear very well. But every morning when he gets up he begins quoting scripture from memory. He sometimes quotes verses for as long as two hours. And those who care for him say that his mind's as sharp as it ever was. He says, too, that he still "hears songs to write," but he can't see how to write them down. He keeps his mind alive and active by constant use. And he will die young someday well over 100 years of age.

In terms of wisdom, (the "know how" to apply knowledge), those who are older have a definite edge over younger people. God knew that, didn't he? He knew that some things should be taught by those who were qualified by age and experience. And he lends grace and honor to them: "Rise in the presence of the aged. Show respect for the elderly" (Leviticus 19:32). I think that's why church leaders are called "elders" in the Bible.

Will Power

Old horse traders will tell you that you can't judge a good horse by looking only at his exterior. You've got to get his mouth open and take a good look at his teeth before you can know if that horse is really a good buy.

You may have noticed that nothing has been said in this book about money, prestige, superior education, good looks or good health. These are not the things that make things right when things go wrong. A vital, growing person may or may not have these insignificant exterior qualities. It is the intrinsic qualities—the heart, the soul, the attitudes and the will of a person — that must grow if he is to be a whole person.

These special intrinsic qualities are developed by the exercise of the will power. A doctor friend of mine recently lamented the death of a mutual friend by saying, "He could have pulled through; he just didn't *will* to."

I think Scott Peck said it best in *The Road Less Traveled*: "I therefore believe that the patient's will to grow is the one crucial determinant of success or failure in psychotherapy. Yet, it is a factor that is not at all understood or even recognized by contemporary psychiatric theory."

SPIRITUAL GROWTH

Spiritually, we can keep on growing and being productive as long as we live. "The righteous flourish like the palm tree . . . They still bring forth fruit in old age . . ." (Psalm 92:12,14). And listen to this: "Therefore we do not lose heart. Though outwardly we are wasting away, yet inwardly we are being renewed day by day. For our light and momentary troubles are achieving for us an eternal glory that far outweighs them all. So we fix our eyes not on what is seen, but on what is unseen. For what is seen is temporary, but what is unseen is eternal. Now we know that if the earthly tent we live in is destroyed, we have a building from God, an eternal house in heaven, not built by human hands" (2 Corinthians 4:16-5:1).

But how do we grow spiritually? The first psalm describes the righteous (spiritual) man as a tree "that yields its fruit in its season, and its leaf does not wither." This verse suggests that there are cycles in the rate of our spiritual growth. There are seasons when we can bear much fruit and other seasons when we struggle just to keep our leaves from withering.

If we could use a graph line to plot the course of our spiritual growth and movement, it would not appear as a vertical line pointing straight toward the heavens. It would more closely resemble a line sloping gradually upward that gives the appearance of the lines on an electrocardiogram chart. There would be peaks and valleys, high points and low points, up times and down times.

DOWN IN THE VALLEY

You need no reminders from me as to what those low points on such a chart would represent. You know that they are the down times in our spiritual life when we're troubled and distressed — just hanging on for dear life to God's grace to sustain us.

Many of life's most valuable lessons are learned, not during our mountain-peak highs, but rather during our death-valley days. Look at King David, for example, as he sits down to write the familiar lines of Psalm 23. We see him writing about some of his own unique experiences, both in the high places and in the low places of life. He descends into the valley of the shadows of sorrow. Depression and death, the enormity of his need and the awareness of his own personal inadequacy engulf him completely.

It was down in that valley where he discovered that God would walk with him even through the valley of death. Even there the Lord was present to provide counsel and assistance. To know that God hadn't abandoned him when he needed him the most, to know that God loved him and was willing to shoulder his burdens was all David needed to know. That was enough. So with a song of praise overflowing his heart, he writes: "The Lord is my shepherd . . . I shall not want."

When I think of people who have experienced the shadows of the valley of death, I think of a preacher friend of mine who for 13 years carried his crippled, cancer-ridden wife around in his arms because he wanted to share his life's experiences with her. He watched her dying slowly before his eyes, her weight diminishing from 128 to 67 pounds at the time of her death. When she died he kissed her head and said, "I've carried my angel for the last time." What a beautiful spirit! Like the Lord, he walked with her in his arms to the valley of death. And, I believe, if he could have, he would have carried her through it.

I think, too, of Beverly. One day she had a beautiful family — a husband, two sons and a daughter. The next day, all of the men in her family were gone. The following day I conducted the funeral. What do you say to a mother and daughter who pause at three caskets to look at their loved ones and then turn and look at you for comfort? Believe me, that's tough. If I didn't have faith in a God who can make things right when they've all gone wrong, there would be nothing to say.

Where was God and what was he doing when my preacher friend lost his wife and Beverly lost her husband and two fine sons? He was there in the valley with them, doing exactly what he promised he would do. "Even to your old age and gray hairs I am he, I am he who will sustain you. I have made you, and I will carry you. I will sustain you, and I will rescue you" (Isaiah 46:4). The valley days can become growth times when we realize that even there, he is with us. He will lead us.

BESSIE

There was a little lady named Bessie in the church in Wellington, New Zealand. She was 86 years old and worked as the church secretary there. She was a spunky little gal with an indomitable spirit. And she kept that church spinning like a top.

The church in Wellington was getting ready for a special door-knocking campaign, and Bessie was working hard to get everything ready for it. But one day on her way home (by the way, she walked about four miles!) she fell and cracked both her ankles. Someone rushed her to the hospital, and the doctor put both feet and ankles in "plaster," as they say in New Zealand.

Well, Bessie was not at all happy about the whole situation. But she didn't let it get her down. She got her some crutches, and away she went to the office every day getting ready for the campaign. Now, what you have to understand is that Wellington is located in the mountains, which drop straight down to sea level and the harbor around which she's built. So, it's tough going. And the church building had a set of about 25 steps up to the first floor. From there it was another flight of stairs up to the office where she worked. And, then, the printing press and duplicating equipment were in the attic, up a set of pull-down, rickety stairs. Did that stop Bessie? Nope.

About a week before the campaign group was to arrive, and before her ankles were completely healed, Bessie went to the doctor. She said, "Doctor, I want you to take this plaster off my legs."

He said, "But, Bessie, your ankles aren't completely healed yet."

To that she answered, "If you don't take it off for me, I'll just go home and chip it off with a chisel and hammer!"

He took it off and replaced it with elastic bandages for more maneuverability. And Bessie went merrily hobbling about her work, up and down the stairs and hills, throughout the three-week campaign. She was incredible! She knew where her strength came from, and she counted on him walking with her through the dark valleys.

RISKS AND THRILLS

Life is risky business. In fact, you can't get out of it alive. But you can't sit around with your hands folded in your lap trying to avoid the consequences of taking a risk either.

It's like the trapeze artists in the circus. They swing back and forth hanging on to the trapeze bar. But if that's all they do, there's no thrill for the audience. It's that split second when the artist lets go of the bar and is "flying through the air with the greatest of ease" that makes the audience stand up and cheer. It's the letting go, taking the risk that the other trapeze will arrive at just the right moment, that gives life excitement.

Sure, the danger of falling is always there. But the guy who clings to the trapeze bar and never lets go cannot know the exhilaration of the guy who releases himself to take the risk. He may live longer, but he won't live better.

ALIVE IN CHRIST

We are *going* to die, you know. No matter how young you may be, you are one day older than you were yesterday and one day nearer the day of your death. You may be beautiful or handsome, but one of these days as the changing process continues you're likely going to get wrinkles on your face, sagging flesh around your throat and neck muscles and dark spots on your hands. You can use cosmetics to cover the skin blemishes. But you are still going to grow old and die. We will *not* come out of this alive. So, you can look at old age as a period of growth and development that is going somewhere better, or you can resent God, the world and yourself and experience all sorts of bitterness.

We who have been made alive in Christ know that we are growing and moving toward somewhere that is far better than anything we've experienced on this earth. So, we do not lose heart just because our physical bodies are deteriorating with each passing day. "We know that if the earthly tent we live in is destroyed, we have a building from God, an eternal house in heaven" (2 Corinthians 5:1).

There are some things in our lives that can become better and stronger with age. Love in marriage is one of those things. Lederer and Jackson discovered in their research that the kind of marriages which they considered to be most satisfying and ideal, that "hand in glove fit" where each partner clearly reads the other's signals, existed *only* between elderly men and women who had lived together for 30 years or more. It doesn't happen quickly.

Who are the most loving and helpful people you know? Old people. They've had more practice. Who are the most hateful and cantankerous people that you know? Old people. They've had more practice. What kind of person will you be in your old age? How you think and act now will determine it.

I am grateful to Elise Maclay for granting me permission to share the following section of her book, *Approaching Autumn*, with you. I think it depicts beautifully what can happen to marriage partners in the autumn years of life.

He Speaks:

How can a man of seventy,
Holder of half a dozen civic offices,
Husband, father, grandfather,
Admit that he
Is terrified of retirement?
At sixty-five I was sure I'd be
Ready to quit at the end
Of the five-year extension they gave me.
Truth to tell, of course,
When I said
In five years I'll go gracefully,
I thought I'd be dead by then,
But I didn't die,
And the years went by
Like the blink of an eye.
My desk calendar
Says the fateful day
Is a month away.
What if I refuse to go?

Chain myself to this chair?
Lock myself in the executive suite?
Picket? Refuse to eat?
Today, for the first time, I
Know how it feels to be
Helpless.
Help.
Help of the helpless,
Oh, abide with me.

She Speaks:

I hate to admit it but I've grown
Quite set in my ways.
How will it be when he's home all the time?
He takes up a lot of room in a room.
Of course, he can be a big help, too,
But where was he when the house was piled high
with toys
And I got chicken pox along with the boys?
Where was he when Jennifer was teething
And Tim broke his hand
And I had to drive somebody somewhere every day?
I know. He had to go to the office,
Had to travel on business. He didn't choose to,
It was all he knew,
And he missed so much:
The clutch of baby fingers,
John learning to swim,
That sturdy little body, glistening in the sun,
Jenny practicing lines for the fifth-grade play,
Music lessons, homework, jokes and games,
Spring, mud on the floor and birds on the wing,
And everything brighter and lighter because the
children were around.
They're grown and gone now
And he missed it all,
How will he fill the time and space now
In this strange place
Called home?
He looks a bit like Tim setting off for kindergarten
With a new book bag and a trembly smile,

Hiding his fear.
Oh God,
Help me run to meet him
And make him feel welcome here.

He Speaks:

We always planned
To take the Grand Tour,
But inflation ate into our savings
And we more or less decided to settle
For back-yard barbecues
And the "National Geographic."
Then we started getting postcards
From the grandchildren:
Amsterdam, Copenhagen, Athens, Rome.
Fantastic. Wow. We may never come home!
"They go everywhere," Molly said, wistfully,
"Without a penny to their name."
Then she said (her eyes sparkling as they hadn't in years),
"Couldn't we do the same?
Fly charter, ride second-class trains,
Stay in pensions, guest houses, rented rooms?
As for food, a roll and coffee will do for breakfast,
Fruit and cheese for lunch,
For dinner, too, if need be."
I couldn't refuse her, though you know
I was scared to death.
Of what?
Of discomfort, I'm ashamed to say,
Of not having things the way
I'm used to having them,
My breakfast egg,
Leg of lamb on Sunday.
The newspaper delivered.
Familiarity is comfortable,
It's also deadening.
I scarcely saw the flowers in our garden;
Today a meadow of poppies and cornflowers
Took my breath away.
Last week,

A snowy alpine peak
Satisfied me as no high-calorie
Meal ever did or could,
Though we missed dinner and the only food
We could find was a loaf of black bread
And a rind of cheese left from lunch.
But munching it at sunset in a field,
Our backs against a rock,
Was peace and joy and poetry,
And my girl was there beside me,
Nibbling cheese, pushing back a lock of curly gray
hair,
Her eyes shining.

She Speaks:

We missed connections last night.
He waited at one train station
And I waited at another.
I was calm at first,
Then panic mounted,
And insight.
I realized how much I counted on him
To give meaning to my life.
If he didn't come,
I didn't want to go home,
Didn't want to go anywhere,
Didn't care about anything.
I kept telling myself, it's nothing,
A traffic jam, his watch is wrong.
I had to wait quietly, composing my face
Because this was a public place,
But terror gripped my throat
And I couldn't catch my breath.
It will be like this, I thought,
At his death,
At his funeral. I cannot rant and tear my hair,
It must be a dignified affair,
Befitting his station. At his age
And mine, resignation is expected.
Who will understand that at seventy,

It is possible to be
More in love than at twenty-three?

THE BEST IS YET TO BE

Old age can be beautiful. The autumn years can be colorful seasons of growth and development in which one continues to produce and achieve as God's plans and purposes are fulfilled in their life. With God in control of your life you can, at every stage of life, continue to grow in your love and devotion to God and others. So choose to die young, no matter how old you are.

Inner security and happiness, at any age, come from a sense of one's own worth and dignity as a child of God. You may be getting old, but if you are a child of God, the best is yet to be! Death isn't the end of your future — it's just the beginning. He has given you "eternal life . . . in his Son" (1 John 4:11). So don't lose heart. "For our light and momentary troubles are achieving for us an eternal glory that far outweighs them all."

THE POWER TO MAKE THINGS RIGHT

God has the power to make things right, even when they've gone all wrong. He can right the wrongs of this world and in your personal life. He has made the things that have gone wrong in my life right through his son and the cross. And he can do the same for you as long as you remain in the love of Christ. By keeping your relationship with him right, you can conquer all the wrongs life can throw at you.

The apostle Paul contemplated this idea when writing to the Christians at Rome during their terrible persecutions: "Who shall separate us from the love of Christ? Shall trouble or hardship or persecution or famine or nakedness or danger or sword?" In other words, folks, what's going to happen when everything goes wrong?

And after thinking about it, Paul was led by God to answer: "No, in all these things we are more than conquerors through him who loved us. For I am convinced that neither death nor life, neither angels not demons, neither the present nor the future, nor any powers, neither height nor depth, nor anything else in all creation, will be able to separate us from the love of God that is in Christ Jesus our Lord" (Romans 8:35,37-39).